$\mathscr{A}$DVENT *and* $\mathscr{C}$HRISTMAS $\mathscr{W}$ISDOM
—— *from* ——
SAINT
THÉRÈSE
OF LISIEUX

Advent and Christmas Wisdom

from

SAINT THÉRÈSE OF LISIEUX

Daily Scripture and Prayers Together
With Saint Thérèse of Lisieux's Own Words

John Cleary

Liguori

Imprimi Potest:
Harry Grile, CSsR, Provincial
Denver Province, The Redemptorists

Published by Liguori Publications
Liguori, Missouri 63057

To order, visit Liguori.org or call 800-325-9521.

Library of Congress Cataloging-in-Publication Data

Cleary, John J.
   Advent & Christmas wisdom from St. Thérèse of Lisieux / John Cleary.—First Edition.
      pages cm
   ISBN 978-0-7648-2172-1
   1. Advent—Prayers and devotions. 2. Christmas—Prayers and devotions. 3. Catholic Church—Prayers and devotions. 4. Thérèse, de Lisieux, Saint, 1873–1897. I. Title. II. Title: Advent and Christmas wisdom from St. Thérèse of Lisieux.
   BX2170.A4C64 2014
   242'.33—dc23
                                        2014030925
p ISBN: 978-0-7648-2172-1
e ISBN: 978-0-7648-6972-3

Quotations at the start of each chapter are from the Project Gutenberg ebook of *The Story of a Soul (L'Histoire d'une Âme): The Autobiography of St. Thérèse of Lisieux*, by Thérèse Martin (of Lisieux). Translator: Thomas Taylor
Additional writings and sayings of St. Thérèse also are included.

Liguori Publications, a nonprofit corporation, is an apostolate of The Redemptorists. To learn more about The Redemptorists, visit Redemptorists.com.

Printed in the United States of America
18 17 16 15 14 / 5 4 3 2 1
First Edition

$\mathcal{C}$ontents

Preface

A Path for Advent and Christmas:
Thérèse's "Little Way"

Thérèse Martin was born in Alençon, France, on January 2, 1873. Two days later, she was baptized Marie Frances Thérèse at Notre Dame Church. Her parents were Louis Martin and Zélie Guérin. After the death of her mother on August 28, 1877, Thérèse and her family moved to Lisieux.

On April 9, 1888, Thérèse entered the Carmel of Lisieux. She received the habit on January 10 of the following year and made her religious profession on September 8, 1890, on the feast of the Birth of the Blessed Virgin Mary.

In Carmel she embraced the way of perfection outlined by the foundress, St. Teresa of Jesus, fulfilling with genuine fervor and fidelity the various community responsibilities entrusted to her. Her faith was tested by the sickness of her beloved father, Louis Martin, who died on July 29, 1894. Thérèse nevertheless grew in sanctity, enlightened by the word of God and inspired by the Gospel to place love at the center of everything. In her autobiographical writings she left us not only her recollections of childhood and adolescence but also a portrait of her soul, the description of her most intimate experiences. She discovered the "little way" of spiritual childhood and taught it to the novices entrusted to her care. Seized by the love of Christ, she became increasingly aware of her apostolic and missionary vocation to draw everyone in her path toward that one love as well.

Her time of trial continued even as her health declined, but new graces led her to perfection, and she discovered fresh insights for the diffusion of her message in the Church for the benefit of souls who would follow her way. Thérèse accepted her sufferings and trials with patience up to the moment of her death on the afternoon of September 30, 1897. Her final words were: "My God, I love you." This simple statement sealed a life that was extinguished at age twenty-four. A short time later, a new phase of apostolic presence on behalf of the souls in the communion of saints was begun, as Thérèse had desired, in order to shower a rain of roses upon the world.

Thérèse was canonized by Pope Pius XI on May 17, 1925.

Both her teachings and example of holiness have been received with great enthusiasm by all sectors of the faithful ever since, as well as by people outside the Catholic Church and outside Christianity.

In view of the soundness of her spiritual wisdom inspired by the Gospel, the originality of her theological intuitions filled with sublime teaching, and the universal acceptance of her spiritual message—which has been welcomed throughout the world and spread by the translation of her works into more than fifty languages—Pope John Paul II proclaimed Thérèse of the Child Jesus a doctor of the Church on World Mission Sunday, October 19, 1997. This is an honor the Catholic Church confers upon a person who has led a notably holy life and helped the propagation of Christian values and thoughts.

St. Thérèse of Lisieux: Made by God, for God. Truer words were never spoken, and while this truth may be lost on us, it was never lost on "The Little Flower." She is a great saint, a precious woman who realized her "littleness" to such a degree that she understood the more she made herself small the closer the Lord would draw her near. In her "little way," Thérèse found the presence of the Lord in the tiniest facets of his creation, in every corner of her experience, in every little thing she said or did. God in all things, indeed! God gave Thérèse everything she had and, in turn, she made it her life's mission to give everything back to him. Made by God, for God.

Throughout this Advent and Christmas journey, we will explore the wellspring that is the spirituality of St. Thérèse of Lisieux, one of the most beloved saints in the long history of the Catholic Church. May her "little way" to the Lord serve as our own path to a greater nearness and devotion to our Savior, and may our loving Jesus draw us closer to him as we contemplate his own Incarnation and birth. Know also, dear readers, that your spiritual growth and welfare is committed to my own prayers as you proceed along this worthy Advent and Christmas journey.

John Cleary
St. Louis, 2014

St. Thérèse of Lisieux

A CHRONOLOGY

1873 • On January 2, Thérèse Martin is born in Alençon, France, to Louis Martin and Zélie Guérin Martin. Two days later, she is baptized Marie Frances Thérèse at Notre Dame Church.

1877 • After the death of her mother on August 28, Thérèse and her family move to Lisieux.

1888 • On the feast of the Annunciation, Thérèse enters the Carmelite convent of Lisieux as a postulant.

1890 • Thérèse makes her profession on the feast of Our Lady's Nativity and, several weeks later, takes the veil.

1894 • Louis Martin dies in July.

1896 • Thérèse finishes writing her autobiography, *The Story of a Soul*, and gives it the prioress, who had ordered her to write her memoirs. Later that year, Thérèse begins coughing up blood and experiences spiritual depression.

1897 • Thérèse becomes seriously ill in April; in July she is taken to the convent infirmary and receives the last sacraments. On September 30, after much suffering, Thérèse dies, surrounded by her community.

1923 • Thérèse is beatified by Pope Pius XI.

1925 • Thérèse of the Child Jesus is canonized by Pope Pius XI on May 17.

1927 • Pope Pius XI names Thérèse Patroness of all Missionaries, together with St. Francis Xavier.

1980 • Pope John Paul II makes a pilgrimage to Lisieux.

1997 • Pope John Paul II proclaims St. Thérèse of Lisieux a doctor of the Church on October 19.

How to Use This Book

Advent—that period of great anticipatory joy—is a time of preparation for the celebration of Jesus' arrival in Bethlehem as a helpless infant. In Western liturgy, Advent begins four Sundays before December 25—the Sunday closest to November 30, which is the feast of St. Andrew, Jesus' first disciple. The four weeks of Advent are often thought of as symbolizing the four different ways that Jesus comes into the world: (1) at his birth as a helpless infant at Bethlehem, (2) at his arrival in the hearts of believers, (3) at his death, and (4) at his arrival on Judgment Day.

The annual commemoration of Jesus' birth begins the Christmas cycle of the liturgical year—a cycle that runs from Christmas Eve to the Sunday after the feast of the Epiphany. In keeping with the unfolding of the message of the liturgical year, this book is designed to be used during the entire period from the First Sunday of Advent to the end of the Christmas cycle.

Each "day" in this book begins with the words of St. Thérèse of Lisieux taken from *The Story of a Soul (L'Histoire d'une Âme): The Autobiography of St. Thérèse of Lisieux*. Following that quotation is an excerpt from Scripture that is related in some way to the beginning quote. Next is a small prayer built on the ideas from the two preceding passages. Finally, I suggest an Advent or Christmas activity as a way to apply the messages to your daily life.

Because Christmas falls on a different day of the week each year, the fourth week of Advent is never finished; it is abruptly, joyously, and solemnly abrogated by the annual coming of Jesus at Christmas.

Christ's Second Coming will also one day abruptly interrupt our sojourn here on earth. Since the calendar dictates the number of days in Advent, this book includes Scripture and meditation readings from St. Thérèse for a full twenty-eight days. These twenty-eight daily readings make up Part I of this book. I suggest you begin at the beginning and, on Christmas, switch to Part II, which contains materials for the twelve days of Christmas. If there are any "extra" entries from Part I, you may read them by doubling up days or by reading two entries on weekends. Alternately, you may skip entries that do not fit within the Advent time frame for a particular year.

Should you wish to enhance your daily meditation further, Part III proposes two optional formats for using each day as part of a longer liturgical observance similar to Night Prayer, combined with a version of the Office of Readings. The purpose of these readings is to enrich the Advent/Christmas/Epiphany season of the liturgical year and set up a means by which individuals, families, or groups can observe the true meaning of the season.

PART I

~

READINGS *for* ADVENT

DAY 1

The Divine Sun Shines on the Smallest Flower

God's Love is made manifest as well in a simple soul which does not resist His grace as in one more highly endowed…. He has created the little child, who knows nothing and can but utter feeble cries, and the poor savage who has only the natural law to guide him, and it is to their hearts that He deigns to stoop. These are the field flowers whose simplicity charms Him; and by His condescension to them Our Saviour shows His infinite greatness. As the sun shines both on the cedar and on the floweret, so the Divine Sun illumines every soul, great and small, and all correspond to His care—just as in nature the seasons are so disposed that on the appointed day the humblest daisy shall unfold its petals.

THE STORY OF A SOUL, I, "EARLIEST MEMORIES"

SCRIPTURE

People were bringing children to him that he might touch them, but the disciples rebuked them. When Jesus saw this he became indignant and said to them, "Let the children come to me; do not prevent them, for the kingdom of God belongs to such as these. Amen, I say to you, whoever does not accept the kingdom of God like a child will not enter it." Then he embraced them and blessed them, placing his hands on them.

MARK 10:13–16

PRAYER

Lord Jesus Christ, you love me exactly as I am. Though I am small and meek in your presence, you love me all the more. It is my smallness that moves you to draw me closer to your heart. You do not allow my shortcomings to provide any distance between us. I cannot reach you, cannot even approach you, through my own efforts. It is your grace alone that unites us. I am but a child—one of those little ones you asked to come closer to you. Move me to view your kingdom with eyes of wonder, like the eyes of a child seeking only comfort from his loving Father. Amen.

ADVENT ACTION

In what ways do your imperfections and weaknesses move you to rely more and more on the love of God? How has this reliance on the Lord grown as you've aged? Does this perspective move you to greater forgiveness of yourself? In what ways? In your reflections throughout the Advent season, consider how Jesus draws you closer when you "make yourself small" and confess your inability to give him all that he asks of you by your will alone. Understand that it is your weakness that allows him to love you to the depths both you and he desire. Reflect on this "little way" to God. How does it suit you?

DAY 2

Go the Extra Mile

To give up one's cloak is, it seems to me, to renounce every right, and to regard oneself as the servant, the slave, of all. Without a cloak it is easier to walk or run, and so the Master adds: "And whosoever shall force thee to go one mile, go with him other two" (Matthew 5:41).

It is therefore not enough for me to give to whoever asks—I ought to anticipate the wish, and show myself glad to be of service; but if anything of mine be taken away, I should show myself glad to be rid of it.

THE STORY OF A SOUL, IX, "THE NIGHT OF THE SOUL"

SCRIPTURE

In every way I have shown you that by hard work of that sort we must help the weak, and keep in mind the words of the Lord Jesus who himself said, "It is more blessed to give than to receive."

ACTS 20:35

Give and gifts will be given to you; a good measure, packed together, shaken down, and overflowing, will be poured into your lap. For the measure with which you measure will in return be measured out to you.

LUKE 6:38

PRAYER

Oh Lord our God, you give us every good thing we need without us having to ask. You are our strength when we tire; you are our nourishment when we hunger; you are our hope when we despair. Fill our hearts with the grace to persevere through any and every struggle; strengthen our resolve to keep our attention focused on your word and act according to its wisdom. When others stumble and fall, move us to lift them up in a spirit of humble service. Help us to understand that by giving to others we are brought ever closer to you through our acts of loving service. Amen.

ADVENT ACTION

Make an effort on this day or the next to go above and beyond in an act of service for another. Where you might ordinarily stop in your service to someone who needs help, make the effort to go the extra mile to share God's love with someone in need. Anticipate what a person might need in a given situation—it might be different than it initially appears. Take time to study the situation, to ask questions of the person in need, and be willing to give the time and energy it takes to *listen*. Often, all people want is someone who will really listen to them and understand what they are feeling.

DAY 3

Have Confidence
in His Infinite Mercy

*F*rom the time of my childhood I felt that one day I should be set free from this land of darkness. I believed it, not only because I had been told so by others, but my heart's most secret and deepest longings assured me that there was in store for me another and more beautiful country—an abiding dwelling-place. I was like Christopher Columbus, whose genius anticipated the discovery of the New World. And suddenly the mists about me have penetrated my very soul and have enveloped me so completely that I cannot even picture to myself this promised country...all has faded away.

THE STORY OF A SOUL, IX, "THE NIGHT OF THE SOUL"

SCRIPTURE

"I shall get up and go to my father and I shall say to him, 'Father, I have sinned against heaven and against you. I no longer deserve to be called your son; treat me as you would treat one of your hired workers.'" So he got up and went back to his father. While he was still a long way off, his father caught sight of him, and was filled with compassion. He ran to his son, embraced him and kissed him. His son said to him, 'Father, I have sinned against heaven and against you; I no longer deserve to be called your son.' But his father ordered his servants, 'Quickly bring the finest robe and put it on him; put a ring on his finger and sandals on his feet. Take the fattened calf and slaughter it. Then let us celebrate with a feast because this son of mine was dead, and has come to life again; he was lost, and has been found.' Then the celebration began.

LUKE 15:18–24

PRAYER

Kind and merciful Father, your generous love is without measure, your mercy knows no bounds. Though I have sinned in myriad ways and offended you with my thoughts and words, action and inaction—still you forgive me. Despite all of my failings, you forgive me and celebrate my return when I come running to you, seeking your mercy. Dear Lord, your ceaseless mercy fills my heart with a confidence in your love; though I fail you at times, I am never overwhelmed with grief or despair at my sin. I know your mercy abounds and there is nothing that can keep us apart. I pray that I might show mercy to those who offend me, reflecting as best as I am able, in my human condition, some measure of the divine love and forgiveness you radiate unceasingly. Amen.

ADVENT ACTION

Spend ten minutes in quiet reflection this evening. Consider those times during the past few weeks when you offended God. In what ways did you fail to love him? Did you sin against him through things you did or said? Things you failed to do or say? When you sinned against God, how do you feel? Were you overwhelmed with grief? Did you despair? Were you unaffected at that moment, only feeling the impact of the sin in retrospect? Were you confident of God's mercy? Did you turn to him with a penitent heart and express your remorse for having offended him? Consider participating in the sacrament of reconciliation during this Advent season. Make it a weekly commitment. Open up completely to God with great confidence in his mercy. See how your relationship deepens through this experience.

DAY 4

God's Love Is Unconditional

*H*ow can a soul so imperfect as mine aspire to the pleni-
tude of Love? What is the key of this mystery? O my only
Friend, why dost Thou not reserve these infinite longings to lofty
souls, to the eagles that soar in the heights? Alas! I am but a poor
little unfledged bird. I am not an eagle, I have but the eagle's eyes
and heart! Yet, notwithstanding my exceeding littleness, I dare
to gaze upon the Divine Sun of Love, and I burn to dart upwards
unto Him! I would fly, I would imitate the eagles; but all that I
can do is to lift up my little wings—it is beyond my feeble power
to soar….With daring self-abandonment there will I remain…my
gaze fixed upon that Divine Sun. Nothing shall affright me, nor
wind nor rain. And should impenetrable clouds conceal the Orb

of Love, and should I seem to believe that beyond this life there is darkness only, that would be the hour of perfect joy, the hour in which to push my confidence to its uttermost bounds. I should not dare to detach my gaze, well knowing that beyond the dark clouds the sweet Sun still shines.

THE STORY OF A SOUL, XI, "A CANTICLE OF LOVE"

SCRIPTURE

He said..., "you shall love the Lord, your God, with all your heart, with all your being, with all your strength, and with all your mind, and your neighbor as yourself."

LUKE 10:27

I live, no longer I, but Christ lives in me; insofar as I now live in the flesh, I live by faith in the Son of God who has loved me and given himself up for me.

GALATIANS 2:20

In this way the love of God was revealed to us: God sent his only Son into the world so that we might have life through him. In this is love: not that we have loved God, but that he loved us and sent his Son as expiation for our sins.

1 JOHN 4:9–10

PRAYER

Oh Lord, my God, you have loved me into being. Without you, all that I am, all the joys that move me to praise you, all the sadness and loneliness that bind me ever closer to you, and every breath of my life from birth to death would never be. I have every confidence that you will hold me close to your loving heart, for you have never wavered in your unconditional love for me, for my neighbor, or for all of humanity throughout the history of our great and enduring covenant of love. I ask that you grace my heart to avoid any temptation that might keep me from you, and I ask this in the name of your Son, my Lord and Savior, Jesus Christ. Amen.

ADVENT ACTION

At the close of this day, as you prepare for sleep, spend ten to fifteen minutes in quiet reflection. Consider the blessings you have received throughout your life to this point. Consider the tragedy, periods of loneliness, and stretches of spiritual dryness that have brought you closer to God. How has the love of God shaped your life? How has God's love moved you to love? In what ways do you share the love of God with those closest to you? With strangers?

As Christmas Day approaches and the anticipation of God's greatest gift fills your heart, how would you like the love of God to further shape your behavior and outlook this Advent season? In what concrete ways can you your love emulate the unconditional love you have known from your heavenly Father?

DAY 5

Find Your Joy in God Alone

I had one other great wish; it was to love God only, and to find my joy in Him alone. During my thanksgiving after Holy Communion I often repeated this passage from the *Imitation of Christ*: "O my God, who art unspeakable sweetness, turn for me into bitterness all the consolations of earth." These words rose to my lips quite naturally; I said them like a child, who, without well understanding, repeats what a friend may suggest. Later on I will tell you...how Our Lord has been pleased to fulfill my desire, how He, and He alone, has always been my joy.

THE STORY OF A SOUL, IV, "FIRST COMMUNION AND CONFIRMATION"

SCRIPTURE

My soul, be at rest in God alone, from whom comes my hope.
God alone is my rock and my salvation, my fortress;
   I shall not fall.
My deliverance and honor are with God, mysterious rock;
   my refuge is with God.
Trust God at all times, my people! Pour out your hearts
   to God our refuge!

PSALM 62:6–9

PRAYER

Loving Father, it is you alone who gives my heart rest, in whom I trust completely and who knows every corner of heart, the depths of my person I have yet to come to know myself. Reveal yourself to me, oh wonderful God, and help me to experience your love in everything I do, every word I speak, and every person I meet. Despite the distractions and temptations that come my way, grace me with the perseverance to rely on you, my rock and my protection. When the deception of those who would do me harm attempts to pull me away from you, hold me close to your heart. Every comfort I desire and all the nourishment I require comes from you, dear Lord. Never let me go. Amen.

ADVENT ACTION

Make daily/nightly reading of the Gospels part of your Advent spiritual routine for growth. Do not attempt to read too large a passage in one sitting. Choose ten verses or less and reflect on every phrase you read. Allow small portions of text, a verse or two at a time, penetrate your heart. Think on these words, pray on them, meditate on them. In what way is God speaking to you through the Scripture you consume? How is he instructing you in how to view the world and those you meet throughout your day, even in affairs that seem mundane? How is he revealing himself to you? How is he revealing yourself to you? Put yourself in the crowd of people who follow and listen to the Lord. Let his words guide you.

DAY 6

I Am Your Child, Lord: Hold Me Close

I entreat you to adopt me as your child. All the glory that you help me to acquire will be yours; only deign to hear my prayer, and obtain for me a double portion of the love of God.

O my God! I cannot measure the extent of my request, I should fear to be crushed by the very weight of its audacity. My only excuse is my claim to childhood, and that children do not grasp the full meaning of their words. Yet if a father or mother were on the throne and possessed vast treasures, they would not hesitate to grant the desires of those little ones, more dear to them than life itself. To give them pleasure they will stoop even unto folly.

Well, I am a child of Holy Church, and the Church is a Queen, because she is now espoused to the Divine King of Kings. I ask not for riches or glory, not even the glory of Heaven—that belongs by right to my brothers the Angels and Saints, and my own glory shall be the radiance that streams from the queenly brow of my Mother, the Church.

THE STORY OF A SOUL, XI, "A CANTICLE OF LOVE"

SCRIPTURE

When Jesus was born in Bethlehem of Judea, in the days of King Herod, behold, magi from the east arrived in Jerusalem, saying, "Where is the newborn king of the Jews? We saw his star at its rising and have come to do him homage." ...After their audience with the king they set out. And behold, the star that they had seen at its rising preceded them, until it came and stopped over the place where the child was. They were overjoyed at seeing the star, and on entering the house they saw the child with Mary his mother. They prostrated themselves and did him homage. Then they opened their treasures and offered him gifts of gold, frankincense, and myrrh.

MATTHEW 2:1–2, 9–11

PRAYER

Heavenly Father, you granted the world the greatest gift it has ever known when you gave us your Son, our Lord Jesus. Your word became flesh, shared our human condition, and sanctified every portion of it. Because of this great gift, Dear

Father, salvation is won for all people, and we are joined with you forever, joined with you beyond death. Move me, generous Lord, to make my gift to you every day as I shine the light of your love upon every person I meet. Work through me, Father. I ask this in the name of your greatest gift, my Lord and Savior, Jesus Christ. Amen.

ADVENT ACTION

During this Advent season, view yourself as a gift to your Lord Jesus by giving yourself to others; you are a gift given by the Father, so that the world might know his love for all. Emulate and imitate Jesus, the Father's greatest gift, by giving yourself generously to those in greatest need. Extend yourself to those who need to know the Lord's love for them the most. You are a gift to the holy Infant, Jesus. You are not gold, frankincense, or myrrh—you are something greater. Reflect on the following before taking action: Who would benefit from my time and attention as a good listener, allowing for another to share their suffering and pain? To whom might I provide comfort, perhaps surprising that person with a meal? Who would benefit from a kind word from me while navigating through a challenging period? See the need and provide for it. Make this your gift to the holy Infant on this day of Advent.

DAY 7

He Has Given Us
the Great Gift of His Mercy

*M*ay I not sing with the Psalmist that "the Lord is good, that His Mercy endureth forever"? (Psalm 103[104]:1)

It seems to me that if everyone were to receive such favours God would be feared by none, but loved to excess; that no one would ever commit the least willful fault—and this through love, not fear.

Yet all souls cannot be alike. It is necessary that they should differ from one another in order that each Divine Perfection may receive its special honour. To me, He has given His Infinite Mercy, and it is in this ineffable mirror that I contemplate his other attributes. Therein all appear to me radiant with Love. His Justice, even more perhaps than the rest, seems to me to be clothed with Love. What joy to think that Our Lord is just, that is to say, that

He takes our weakness into account, that He knows perfectly the frailty of our nature! Of what, then, need I be afraid?

THE STORY OF A SOUL, VIII, "PROFESSION OF SOEUR THÉRÈSE"

SCRIPTURE

For the Son of Man has come to save what was lost. What is your opinion? If a man has a hundred sheep and one of them goes astray, will he not leave the ninety-nine in the hills and go in search of the stray? And if he finds it, amen, I say to you, he rejoices more over it than over the ninety-nine that did not stray. In just the same way, it is not the will of your heavenly Father that one of these little ones be lost.

MATTHEW 18:11–14

PRAYER

Good and faithful God, Father of love: you know my every need; you know my every fault; my every fault brings me ever closer to you as you seek to tend my wound and make me whole. You know me at my core; there is no weakness I can keep from you. And praise be that I am known completely to you! Your mercy knows no bounds! You created me as I am, complete with all my faults, and you love me, warts and all. When I stray from your flock, oh loving Shepherd, I am filled with the comfort that you will seek me out and, finding me, you will hold me even closer than before. For this—and so much more—I praise your name. Amen.

ADVENT ACTION

Take ten or fifteen minutes tonight or in the morning. Find a quiet place for reflection—just you, your thoughts, and God. Consider the great mercy the Lord has shown you throughout your life. Look into your past upon those times you fell or failed to act in accordance with his will. Do not view these moments through the lens of guilt. God does not want his beloved creation to wallow in self-hatred or in the stagnation of guilt. Instead, view the faults of your past with a glad heart and with a sense of gratitude for the mercy the Lord has shown in loving you all the more, in spite of your faults, because of your faults. How have these moments of mercy shaped your love for God? How have these moments of mercy shaped your own willingness to be merciful of others? View every one of these moments with gratitude for the grace you have been given.

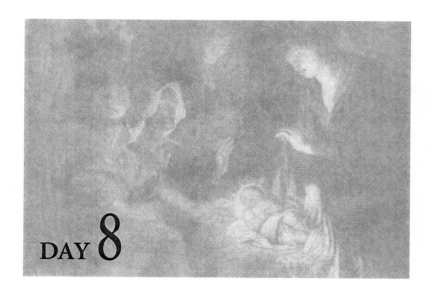

DAY 8

The Word of God Sustains Me

*I*t may be that some day my present state will appear to me full of defects, but nothing now surprises me, and I do not even distress myself because I am so weak. On the contrary I glory therein, and expect each day to find fresh imperfections. Nay, I must confess, these lights on my own nothingness are of more good to my soul than lights on matters of Faith. Remembering that "Charity covereth a multitude of sins" (Proverbs 10:12), I draw from this rich mine, which Our Saviour has opened to us in the Gospels. I search the depths of His adorable words, and cry out with David: "I have run in the way of Thy commandments since Thou hast enlarged my heart" (Psalm 118:32).

THE STORY OF A SOUL, IX, "THE NIGHT OF THE SOUL"

Scripture

Therefore, since we have been justified by faith, we have peace with God through our Lord Jesus Christ, through whom we have gained access (by faith) to this grace in which we stand, and we boast in hope of the glory of God. Not only that, but we even boast of our afflictions, knowing that affliction produces endurance, and endurance, proven character, and proven character, hope, and hope does not disappoint, because the love of God has been poured out into our hearts through the holy Spirit that has been given to us.

ROMANS 5:1–5

Prayer

Source of all hope, you who bestow all graces upon your beloved creation, Father, Son, and Holy Spirit, guide me to follow your will and commit my life to serving your will. You are the cradle that I desire, as I am but your small child who seeks to praise your holy name in every small effort I make. Even my most mundane actions—smiling toward a stranger, washing the dishes, tending to my garden—let them glorify you as I keep you in mind throughout my day. Let me commit every breath in praise of your name, and may you draw me ever closer to you. Grace me, I ask of you, grace me with perseverance in my efforts to know you to the greatest depths. Amen.

ADVENT ACTION

Devote ten to fifteen minutes this evening or tomorrow morning to reading Scripture. Specifically, read the Gospel passage from Luke 8:4–17. Imagine yourself standing beside Jesus; imagine that he is speaking directly to you. What do these words of the Lord mean to you? How are you moved by the word of God? Does it fill you with hope? Does it inspire you to persevere and glorify God's name through your words and actions? How do you view the more mundane periods of your day? Can you find God in every little thing? Can you follow the path of Thérèse's "Little Way," committing every aspect of your day—even for an hour—to complete devotion to your Lord? Make your very existence a celebration of his love and feel yourself drawn ever closer to his heart.

DAY 9

I Delight in the Sweetness of Charity

And charity alone can make wide the heart. O Jesus! Since its sweet flame consumes my heart, I run with delight in the way of Thy New Commandment, and I desire to run therein until that blessed day when, with Thy company of Virgins, I shall follow Thee through Thy boundless Realm, singing Thy New Canticle—The Canticle of Love.

THE STORY OF A SOUL, IX, "THE NIGHT OF THE SOUL"

SCRIPTURE

My children, I will be with you only a little while longer. You will look for me, and as I told the Jews, "Where I go you cannot come," so now I say it to you. I give you a new commandment: love one another. As I have loved you, so you also should love one another. This is how all will know that you are my disciples, if you have love for one another.

JOHN 13:33–35

PRAYER

God of love, there is nothing so sweet as charity! It is your love that makes this world go around—you loved the universe into creation, you loved the earth into being, and you loved each and every person into life. Everything we are begins with your love. Our ability to share in your love by loving others is a gift from you as well. Grace me, dear Lord, and allow me to know your love to the greatest depths. Grace me, loving Father, and use me as your instrument. May every person I meet this Advent season know the sweetness of your charity as it radiates through my every word and action. I ask this through your Son, our Lord Jesus Christ. Amen.

ADVENT ACTION

Set aside ten to fifteen minutes for reflection this evening. Consider the many ways in which God has loved you throughout your life to this point. In what ways has he shown you love? In what ways does he call you to love him? How, during this Advent season, might you show your love for the Lord in new and creative ways? Does your church offer new and different forms of worship in which you might participate? Can you adopt some forms of worship that you don't normally do? Perhaps saying the rosary or the Chaplet of The Divine Mercy? How might you expand your service to others as you love God at deeper levels? Does your church offer any opportunities? Is there a form of service you would like to try that you've never attempted before? Perhaps volunteering at a soup kitchen or visiting shut-ins. Consider the possibilities.

DAY 10

We Are All Called to Serve the Lord in Our Own Way

I read on, and found comfort in this counsel: "Be zealous for the better gifts. And I show unto you a yet more excellent way." (1 Corinthians 12:31) The Apostle then explains how all perfect gifts are nothing without Love, that Charity is the most excellent way of going surely to God. At last I had found rest.

Meditating on the mystical Body of Holy Church, I could not recognise myself among any of its members as described by St. Paul, or was it not rather that I wished to recognise myself in all? Charity provided me with the key to my vocation.

THE STORY OF A SOUL, XI, "A CANTICLE OF LOVE"

SCRIPTURE

There are different kinds of spiritual gifts but the same Spirit; there are different forms of service but the same Lord; there are different workings but the same God who produces all of them in everyone. To each individual the manifestation of the Spirit is given for some benefit. To one is given through the Spirit the expression of wisdom; to another the expression of knowledge according to the same Spirit; to another faith by the same Spirit; to another gifts of healing by the one Spirit; to another mighty deeds; to another prophecy; to another discernment of spirits; to another varieties of tongues; to another interpretation of tongues. But one and the same Spirit produces all of these, distributing them individually to each person as he wishes.

1 CORINTHIANS 12:4–11

PRAYER

Good and generous God, you give to each of us special gifts by which we might praise your name and spread your good news. Some of us speak well and preach the Gospel according to that gift. Others write well to do the same. Some of us are good listeners, others serve with great energy. Some of us are artists, others comfort with great skill. Each gift a person has from you allows him or her to make you known by that very gift. Help me to find that special gift within me. Tell me how to best use that gift for the sake of love. Move my heart to extend my gift to those in greatest need so that they may know your love through me, your willing vessel. I ask this in the name of your greatest gift, the gift I anticipate during this Advent season, our Lord Jesus Christ. Amen.

ADVENT ACTION

Make time this evening or at some point in your day tomorrow for ten or fifteen minutes of quiet reflection. Consider these questions: What are the greatest gifts the Lord God has given specifically to you? What talents do you have? What things do you do well, either in your own eyes or in the eyes of others? In what ways do you exhibit these gifts? How are you able to share God's love with others through these gifts?

In what ways do your gifts praise the name of God and spread the Good News of the Gospels? How has the Lord called you to serve him in a way that is unique to you? How has the Lord called you to serve him in a way that is similar to others?

DAY 11

It Is God's Grace That Empowers Me

"Give me a lever and a fulcrum on which to lean it," said Archimedes, "and I will lift the world."

What he could not obtain because his request had only a material end, without reference to God, the Saints have obtained in all its fullness. They lean on God Almighty's power itself and their lever is the prayer that inflames with love's fire. With this lever they have raised the world—with this lever the Saints of the Church Militant still raise it, and will raise it to the end of time.

THE STORY OF A SOUL, XI, "A CANTICLE OF LOVE"

SCRIPTURE

Do you not know?

Have you not heard?

The LORD is God from of old,

creator of the ends of the earth.

He does not faint or grow weary,

and his knowledge is beyond scrutiny.

He gives power to the faint,

abundant strength to the weak.

Though young men faint and grow weary,

and youths stagger and fall,

They that hope in the LORD will renew their strength,

they will soar on eagles' wings;

They will run and not grow weary,

walk and not grow faint.

ISAIAH 40:28–31

One thing God has said; two things I have heard:

Strength belongs to God; so too, my Lord, does mercy,

For you repay each man according to his deeds.

PSALM 62:12–13

PRAYER

God of infinite power and merciful healing, without you I am without energy, I am without the power to share your love with my neighbor and the stranger. Fortify me, loving Father, as only you can; grace me with the power to move the hearts of others; shine your love through me, act through me, and allow me to overcome every obstacle that keeps me from serving your will. It is through service to your will that I better understand your love and am better able to convey your love to my brothers and sisters. I ask for your grace in the name of your Son, our Lord Jesus Christ. Amen.

ADVENT ACTION

When you wake tomorrow morning or another morning this week, consider the coming activities of your day. Some—business meetings where you will make a presentation, opening your heart to another, or speaking candidly to a friend who needs to face a difficult situation in his or her life—can create anxiety. Pray for the strength of God your Father before you rise from bed. Ask him for the energy and the guidance to listen and love in your dealings with others.

Imagine yourself in the situations you will face later in the day and understand that God will be with you through it all, strengthening you with his immense power, and gracing you with the words to say and the actions to take. Allow God in his Holy Spirit to operate through you and know that you are not alone.

DAY 12

Whatever Prevents You From Loving Must Be Discarded

I was far from meriting all the graces which Our Lord showered on me. I had a constant and ardent desire to advance in virtue, but often my actions were spoilt by imperfections. My extreme sensitiveness made me almost unbearable. All arguments were useless. I simply could not correct myself in this miserable fault. How, then, could I hope soon to be admitted to the Carmel? A miracle on a small scale was needed to give me strength of character all at once.

THE STORY OF A SOUL, V, "VOCATION OF THÉRÈSE"

SCRIPTURE

If your hand or foot causes you to sin, cut it off and throw it away. It is better for you to enter into life maimed or crippled than with two hands or two feet to be thrown into eternal fire. And if your eye causes you to sin, tear it out and throw it away. It is better for you to enter into life with one eye than with two eyes to be thrown into fiery Gehenna.

MATTHEW 18:8–9

PRAYER

God of love, keep me centered on your will. As you have loved me into existence, may I share your love to all the ends of the earth, beginning at my home, at my work, and in my otherwise routine activities—may this love ripple to the four corners of the globe. When I face temptation, or any distraction that keeps me from knowing the pleasure of your peace and the joy of your love, grace my life with a bridge that guides me over those troubled waters and brings me closer to you by my continued service to your will in every small step I take along the daily path to joining you in everlasting life. I ask this all in the name of your Son, my Lord Jesus Christ. Amen.

ADVENT ACTION

As you approach the joy of Christmas Day and the celebration of God's gift of his Son for the sake of our salvation, make a point of recognizing those temptations and distractions that confront you in your daily life. As you come across every opportunity to love others who cross your path during your day, be aware of the temptations that accompany it—glorifying yourself ("clashing a cymbal") as you perform acts of kindness, turning yourself away from the face of Jesus (the person in need) who crosses your path, or going through the motions of serving the Lord without faith in his love. Keep your focus on the Lord and his will in every moment of your day; drop every distraction that confronts you; and pray that God graces you by keeping you from all temptations in service to his will.

DAY 13

May I Seek Only to Do the Will of My Father

Among the numberless graces that I have received this year, not the least is an understanding of how far-reaching is the precept of charity. I had never before fathomed these words of Our Lord: "The second commandment is like to the first: Thou shalt love thy neighbour as thyself" (Matthew 22:39). I had set myself above all to love God, and it was in loving Him that I discovered the hidden meaning of these other words: "It is not those who say, Lord, Lord! who enter into the Kingdom of Heaven, but he who does the Will of My Father" (see Matthew 7:21).

THE STORY OF A SOUL, IX, "THE NIGHT OF THE SOUL"

SCRIPTURE

[B]y their fruits you will know them. Not everyone who says to me, "Lord, Lord," will enter the kingdom of heaven, but only the one who does the will of my Father in heaven. Many will say to me on that day, "Lord, Lord, did we not prophesy in your name? Did we not drive out demons in your name? Did we not do mighty deeds in your name?" Then I will declare to them solemnly, "I never knew you. Depart from me, you evildoers."

Everyone who listens to these words of mine and acts on them will be like a wise man who built his house on rock. The rain fell, the floods came, and the winds blew and buffeted the house. But it did not collapse; it had been set solidly on rock. And everyone who listens to these words of mine but does not act on them will be like a fool who built his house on sand. The rain fell, the floods came, and the winds blew and buffeted the house. And it collapsed and was completely ruined.

MATTHEW 7:20–27

PRAYER

Loving and faithful God, you who are always there when people need you the most, hold me close to your heart and never let me stray. Should I ever be tempted to try to build upon a faulty foundation by following something I deem more fulfilling than you, draw me back from the brink and turn my eyes from the false promises made to me by the dark one. You are my foundation of rock, strong always and never wavering despite the gusts of wind that threaten my peace.

Help me know your love evermore as I bring your love to my neighbor, he or she who would most benefit from your comfort and security. I ask this in the name of your Son, our Lord Jesus Christ. Amen.

ADVENT ACTION

Spend ten to fifteen minutes in quiet reflection and consider the following questions: In what ways do I love others as I love myself? Do I give people the kindness and comfort I would like to have from others? Do I give people the encouragement and support I would prefer to receive from another? In order to love others I must first love myself. That is sometimes taken for granted, that a person loves himself or herself.

In what ways do I love myself? Do I care for my body and mind through exercise, a good diet, and nourishing reading? Do I fill my mind with encouraging and supportive thoughts when I face challenging or difficult times? In what ways might I improve the ways I love and care for myself?

DAY 14

As the Lord Has Given to Us, So We Give to Others

*O*ne cold winter evening…I heard in the distance the harmonious strains of music outside the convent walls. I pictured a drawing room, brilliantly lighted and decorated, and richly furnished. Young ladies, elegantly dressed, exchanged a thousand compliments, as is the way of the world. Then I looked on the poor invalid I was tending. Instead of sweet music I heard her complaints, instead of rich gilding I saw the brick walls of our bare cloister, scarcely visible in the dim light. The contrast was very moving. Our Lord so illuminated my soul with the rays of truth, before which the pleasures of the world are but as darkness[.]

THE STORY OF A SOUL, X, "THE NEW COMMANDMENT"

SCRIPTURE

As each one has received a gift, use it to serve one another as good stewards of God's varied grace. Whoever preaches, let it be with the words of God; whoever serves, let it be with the strength that God supplies, so that in all things God may be glorified through Jesus Christ, to whom belong glory and dominion forever and ever. Amen.

1 PETER 4:10–11

So when he...washed their feet (and) put his garments back on and reclined at table again, he said to them, "Do you realize what I have done for you? You call me 'teacher' and 'master,' and rightly so, for indeed I am. If I, therefore, the master and teacher, have washed your feet, you ought to wash one another's feet. I have given you a model to follow, so that as I have done for you, you should also do."

JOHN 13:12–15

PRAYER

God of immense love, you who humbled yourself in every way through the Incarnation, you who love me as I am, move me to see your face, the face of Jesus, know your love, and praise your name in every facet of my day. From making breakfast to taking out the trash, from sharing pleasantries with my neighbor to buying groceries, from cleaning the bathroom to encountering a person in need on the street, may I praise your name in all that I do, may I see your face in everyone I meet. You are present everywhere, dear Lord, not just in the sweet smell of flowers but also in the dirty hands of those who seek my help. Help me to see you everywhere. I ask this in the name of Jesus. Amen.

ADVENT ACTION

During this evening or the next, look back on your day and "retrace your steps," remembering each facet of your day as it progressed from the moment you awoke—what you did, what you said, who you met, how you interacted with others. How did you view those moments then? As grace-filled? How do you view them now? Differently? Were there opportunities that presented themselves throughout your day to love others or the Lord at greater depths? Did you make the most of these opportunities, if you saw them then? If you see them in retrospect, make a point of enjoying the presence of God and learning how to share that presence with others at a later date.

DAY 15

A Humble Heart Is a Worthy Gift to the Lord

I am but a weak and helpless child, yet it is my very weakness which makes me dare to offer myself, O Jesus, as victim to Thy Love.

In olden days pure and spotless holocausts alone were acceptable to the Omnipotent God. Nor could His Justice be appeased, save by the most perfect sacrifices. But the law of fear has given place to the law of love, and Love has chosen me, a weak and imperfect creature, as its victim. Is not such a choice worthy of God's Love? Yea, for in order that Love may be fully satisfied, it must stoop even unto nothingness, and must transform that nothingness into fire. O my God, I know it. "Love is repaid by love alone" (St. John of the Cross). Therefore I have sought, I have found, how to ease my heart, by rendering Thee love for love.

THE STORY OF A SOUL, XI, "A CANTICLE OF LOVE"

SCRIPTURE

"On that day you will realize that I am in my Father and you are in me and I in you. Whoever has my commandments and observes them is the one who loves me. And whoever loves me will be loved by my Father, and I will love him and reveal myself to him."

Judas, not the Iscariot, said to him, "Master, (then) what happened that you will reveal yourself to us and not to the world?"

Jesus answered and said to him, "Whoever loves me will keep my word, and my Father will love him, and we will come to him and make our dwelling with him."

JOHN 14:20–23

PRAYER

Triune God—Father, Son, and Holy Spirit—you are perfect unity in your separate persons; unite me to you as I adhere to your holy word. As I embrace your word and live my life by its law, emulating the love and wisdom of my Lord Jesus that I find within, draw me ever closer to your heart, unite me to your will, and grace me with the perseverance to serve you in all that I do. Humble my heart, dear Lord, and in the recognition of my smallness help me to understand that without you I am nothing, Accept my humble heart, loving Lord, as an offering of my love. I ask all of this in the name of your Son, my Lord Jesus Christ. Amen.

ADVENT ACTION

Spend ten to fifteen minutes this evening or just after you wake tomorrow morning in quiet reflection. Consider what the Lord has given you in his holy Scripture. In what ways does the word of God guide you in your life? What books of the Bible especially touch your heart and bring you closer to God. As you anticipate the coming of his Son on Christmas Day, what stories from Scripture fill your heart with joy and inspire you to live your life according to the will of the Father? What words from Jesus move you to humble your heart for the strength of his guidance and the comfort of his peace? Take some time to converse with the Lord. Tell him why his word moves you to love him at greater depths.

DAY 16

Let Your Light Shine for the Lord

I know now that true charity consists in bearing all our neigh-
bours' defects—not being surprised at their weakness, but
edified at their smallest virtues. Above all I know that charity must
not remain shut up in the heart, for "No man lighteth a candle,
and putteth it in a hidden place, nor under a bushel; but upon a
candlestick, that they who come in may see the light" (Luke 11:33).

It seems to me, dear Mother, this candle represents that charity
which enlightens and gladdens, not only those who are dear to us,
but all those who are of the household.

THE STORY OF A SOUL, IX, "THE NIGHT OF THE SOUL"

SCRIPTURE

Take care not to perform righteous deeds in order that people may see them; otherwise, you will have no recompense from your heavenly Father. When you give alms, do not blow a trumpet before you, as the hypocrites do in the synagogues and in the streets to win the praise of others. Amen, I say to you, they have received their reward. But when you give alms, do not let your left hand know what your right is doing, so that your almsgiving may be secret. And your Father who sees in secret will repay you.

MATTHEW 6:1–4

PRAYER

God of love, you who is worthy of all praise, let your love shine through me, and may every person I meet know your love by knowing me. Grace me with courage to shine your love on every person I meet. Grace me with the humility to seek only the reward you provide. May I never seek to glorify myself through my actions, but may it be your name alone to whom people sing praise when they see the light of love I shine, the light of love that has you as its source. Amen.

ADVENT ACTION

At some point during this day or early tomorrow, praise the Lord God through your action; provide a "random act of kindness" to someone in need. Pay a compliment to someone so as to brighten that person's day; shine God's love upon him by letting him know of your admiration for a God-given quality they bear. Encourage someone in need of support. Let him know that you are with him during this difficult time. Let the Lord guide you in your actions. As this quote, often attributed to St. Francis of Assisi, so beautifully put it: "Preach the Gospel at all times, and when necessary, use words."

DAY 17

A Little Way to God, Short and Straight

*I*nstead of being discouraged, I concluded that God would not inspire desires which could not be realised, and that I may aspire to sanctity in spite of my littleness. For me to become great is impossible. I must bear with myself and my many imperfections; but I will seek out a means of getting to Heaven by a little way—very short and very straight, a little way that is wholly new. We live in an age of inventions; nowadays the rich need not trouble to climb the stairs, they have lifts instead. Well, I mean to try and find a lift by which I may be raised unto God, for I am too tiny to climb the steep stairway of perfection.

THE STORY OF A SOUL, IX, "THE NIGHT OF THE SOUL"

SCRIPTURE

He made from one the whole human race to dwell on the entire surface of the earth, and he fixed the ordered seasons and the boundaries of their regions, so that people might seek God, even perhaps grope for him and find him, though indeed he is not far from any one of us. For "In him we live and move and have our being," as even some of your poets have said, "For we too are his offspring." Since therefore we are the offspring of God, we ought not to think that the divinity is like an image fashioned from gold, silver, or stone by human art and imagination.

ACTS 17:26–29

PRAYER

Father of heaven, you cast your eyes upon this humble creature who lives day to day upon the beauty of the earth. God of compassion, through the Incarnation you know well the pain and suffering a human being experiences during his or her life. Source of all love, you created me in love to love you in all that I do. I know that you love me deeply and that your greatest desire is to have me near you, to follow your will, and join you in heaven on my dying day. Make straight my path to you, loving Father, raise up this humble creature who cannot do it on his or her own. I need your grace, Lord. You have sanctified humanity through the life and death of your Son. I am made in your image, loving God; I ask that you unite this creature with his or her Creator. I ask this in the name of your Son, my Lord Jesus. Amen.

ADVENT ACTION

Take a few moments this evening or when you wake the next morning, go into the bathroom, and study your face in the mirror. Look over every aspect of your face—its wrinkles, freckles, moles, birthmarks, pimples, scars, scratches, hair, and everything else. Look yourself in the eyes and tell yourself, "I love you." Say it again and again, at least ten times, each time looking yourself straight in the eyes. Understand that you have been made in God's image. Know that God has made you in his love to be loved and to love him through your service and love to others. God sanctified the human condition through the Incarnation when he made himself man in the person of Jesus on Christmas Day. He sanctified all aspects of the human condition, including death. Love yourself first. Love the face of Jesus looking back at you from the mirror.

DAY 18

The Lord Loves You as a Friend

*J*esus revealed me this Will when at the Last Supper He gave His New Commandment in telling His Apostles to "love one another as He had loved them" (see John 13:34). I set myself to find out how He had loved His Apostles; and I saw that it was not for their natural qualities, for they were ignorant men, full of earthly ideas. And yet He calls them His Friends, His Brethren; He desires to see them near Him in the Kingdom of His Father, and in order to admit them to this Kingdom He wills to die on the Cross, saying: "Greater love than this no man hath, that a man lay down his life for his friends" (John 15:12).

THE STORY OF A SOUL, IX, "THE NIGHT OF THE SOUL"

YOU WERE CHOSEN BY GOD

This is my commandment: love one another as I love you. No one has greater love than this, to lay down one's life for one's friends. You are my friends if you do what I command you. I no longer call you slaves, because a slave does not know what his master is doing. I have called you friends, because I have told you everything I have heard from my Father. It was not you who chose me, but I who chose you and appointed you to go and bear fruit that will remain, so that whatever you ask the Father in my name he may give you. This I command you: love one another.

JOHN 15:12–17

PRAYER

God of friendship, you have shown us what it means to be a true and loving friend to others. By the gift of your Son, Jesus Christ, on Christmas Day, you shared with us the greatest of all gifts any friend could give to another—eternal life in heaven, forever by your side. As a friend to others, you guide me in wisdom to give others my presence, my comfort, my caring, and every gift I have. All of the gifts I give to my friend are from you, and the gifts I share with my friend praise your name and your goodness as I reflect your love as an instrument of your loving will. Grace me with the courage and perseverance to give myself completely to my friends so that they may know your love for them. Amen.

ADVENT ACTION

Take time today or tomorrow to write a "friendship letter" to a friend. Let this person know how much he or she means to you, in what ways he or she brightens your life. List some of the memories you cherish of your friendship with this person. Tell your friend the qualities that you admire in him or her. Tell your friend the ways in which he or she brings you closer to God, that is, what qualities does your friend have that best model to you the love of God for his creation? Tell your friend that you are always there for him or her if your friend is ever in need. Finally, thank your friend for the joy he or she brings to you whenever you share his or her company. Mail this to your friend. It might mean more to him or her than you will ever know. In doing this small act of kindness, you will be sharing the love of God with your friend.

DAY 19

It Is God's Mercy That Matters, Not Our Judgment

From afar it seems so easy to do good to souls, to teach them to love God more, and to model them according to one's own ideas. But, when we draw nearer, we quickly feel that without God's help this is quite as impossible as to bring back the sun when once it has set. We must forget ourselves, and put aside our tastes and ideas, and guide souls not by our own way, but along the path which Our Lord points out.

THE STORY OF A SOUL, X, "THE NEW COMMANDMENT"

SCRIPTURE

Therefore, you are without excuse, every one of you who passes judgment. For by the standard by which you judge another you condemn yourself, since you, the judge, do the very same things. We know that the judgment of God on those who do such things is true. Do you suppose, then, you who judge those who engage in such things and yet do them yourself, that you will escape the judgment of God? Or do you hold his priceless kindness, forbearance, and patience in low esteem, unaware that the kindness of God would lead you to repentance? By your stubbornness and impenitent heart, you are storing up wrath for yourself for the day of wrath and revelation of the just judgment of God, who will repay everyone according to his works: eternal life to those who seek glory, honor, and immortality through perseverance in good works[.]

ROMANS 2:1–7

PRAYER

God of mercy and unconditional love, grace me with humility and compassion when I encounter someone in whom I recognize my own flaws. Move my heart not to freeze with contempt for the weakness and sinfulness of those who share my faults. Allow me to see the face of Christ in every face, and allow my heart to warm to all despite the presence of the sins I despise. You are filled with such tremendous mercy, Lord, and you love the sinner beyond his sin. Grace me to do the same. In loving the other who shares my sinfulness and my flaws I will come to love myself in the same manner. Through showing this love and mercy to myself I will share with you the mercy you radiate, and the circle of love will be shared by you, me, and another. I ask this in the name of your Son, my Lord Jesus Christ. Amen.

ADVENT ACTION

Spend ten to fifteen minutes this evening or sometime tomorrow in quiet reflection. Call to mind a person you know of whom you are especially critical or judgmental. What is it about this person that fills you with such negative emotions? Is it perhaps that he or she shares the same flaws as you? If so, consider the good qualities this person possesses and weigh those God-given gifts against the faults you recognize in him or her. If you struggle to find even one good quality in that person, reflect on how much God loves him or her. Picture the face of Jesus on that person—after all, even that person was created in the image of God. Does your impression of this person change when you realize how much God loves him or her despite the flaws? Does your impression of yourself change when you realize the great mercy God has on you despite your flaws? Make a point of encouraging this person the next time you see him or her. God loves that person—you can, too. Pray for God's grace to do so.

DAY 20

The Lord Shares
My Desire for Communion

I had made it my practice to go to Communion as often as my confessor allowed me, but never to ask for leave to go more frequently. Now, however, I should act differently, for I am convinced that a soul ought to disclose to her director the longing she has to receive her God. He does not come down from Heaven each day in order to remain in a golden ciborium, but to find another Heaven—the Heaven of our souls in which He takes such delight.

Our Lord, Who knew my desire, inspired my confessor to allow me to go to Communion several times a week, and this permission, coming as it did straight from Him, filled me with joy.

THE STORY OF A SOUL, V, "VOCATION OF THÉRÈSE"

SCRIPTURE

Jesus said to them, "Amen, amen, I say to you, unless you eat the flesh of the Son of Man and drink his blood, you do not have life within you. Whoever eats my flesh and drinks my blood has eternal life, and I will raise him on the last day. For my flesh is true food, and my blood is true drink. Whoever eats my flesh and drinks my blood remains in me and I in him. Just as the living Father sent me and I have life because of the Father, so also the one who feeds on me will have life because of me. This is the bread that came down from heaven. Unlike your ancestors who ate and still died, whoever eats this bread will live forever."

JOHN 6:53–58

PRAYER

God of unending love and eternal joy, I praise your name in every way for the gift you give to me in the sacrament of holy Communion. The gift of your Body and Blood in the form of bread and wine unites me to you to depths one could never even imagine. It is your desire that we are joined in this way, and I give thanks to you for loving me to the extent that you would make such a sacrifice. Your word was made flesh and came to us on Christmas Day. The Incarnation, that blessed and miraculous event, united the human and the divine, making possible the salvation of humankind. Praise your name for this kindness, gentle and loving Father! Move my heart to desire you all the more, to embrace you in the Eucharist whenever the opportunity presents itself. Amen.

ADVENT ACTION

Have you ever stopped to reflect on the miracle of the Incarnation? On the beauty of the Eucharist? God becoming one of us is the greatest gift for which humankind could ever think to ask. The sacrament of holy Communion unites us with God in a manner that graces us, nourishes us, and transforms us all at one time. The next time you attend Mass, make it a point to focus your attention on every word of the Eucharistic Prayer. Listen closely as the celebrant offers the Eternal Sacrifice on behalf of the congregation. What do the words tell you? Do they tell you about a God who loves his creation so much that he was willing to become one of them, sanctify their existence in every way, and forever unite himself with them, beyond even the reach of death? Once you return to your pew after consuming the Body and Blood of our Lord, say a prayer of thanksgiving for the gift God has given to you in the form of the holy Eucharist. Share in the same joy Thérèse experienced when she went to Mass!

DAY 21

What We Create Should Please the Lord

$\mathscr{A}$fter having contemplated the works of God, I turned next to admire those of His creatures. Milan was the first Italian town we visited, and we carefully studied its Cathedral of white marble, adorned with countless statues. Céline and I left the timid ones, who hid their faces in fear after climbing to the first stage, and, following the bolder pilgrims, we reached the top, from whence we viewed the city below. When we came down we started on the first of our expeditions; these lasted the whole month of the pilgrimage, and quite cured me of a desire to be always lazily riding in a carriage.

The *"Campo Santo"* [Cemetery] charmed us. The whole vast enclosure is covered with marble statues, so exquisitely carved as to be lifelike, and placed with an apparent negligence that only enhances their charm. You feel almost tempted to console the imaginary personages that surround you, their expression so exactly portrays a calm and Christian sorrow. And what works of art! Here is a child putting flowers on its father's grave—one forgets how solid is marble—the delicate petals appear to slip through its fingers. Sometimes the light veils of the widows, and the ribbons of the young girls, seem floating on the breeze.

THE STORY OF A SOUL, VI, "A PILGRIMAGE TO ROME"

SCRIPTURE

Hallelujah! Praise God in his holy sanctuary;
give praise in the mighty dome of heaven.
Give praise for his mighty deeds,
praise him for his great majesty.
Give praise with blasts upon the horn,
praise him with harp and lyre.
Give praise with tambourines and dance,
praise him with strings and pipes.
Give praise with crashing cymbals,
praise him with sounding cymbals.
Let everything that has breath give praise to the LORD!
Hallelujah!

PSALM 150:1–6

PRAYER

God of love, you have given humankind many great gifts. Some of us are painters, sculptors, and writers; some of us are chefs and gardeners; some of us sing and some of us dance. Whatever gifts we have been given by you, dear Lord, we in turn give to you in praise of your name. Grace me to praise you in every action I make and in every word I say. May my entire day be a prayer of praise and devotion to you, Lord. Grace my special gifts, those things I do very well, with a divine attraction; that is, make it possible that my gifts draw others closer to you when they see your loving presence in what I create in praise of your name. I ask this in the name of your Son, my Lord Jesus Christ. Amen.

ADVENT ACTION

Are you a creator? An artist of any type? You could be a writer, a painter, a chef, a singer, a dancer, anything. Take some time later this evening or tomorrow morning and create something special according to your unique skill, a "gift" for the Baby Jesus in celebration of his coming birthday. Use your special skill to praise the Lord. If you believe you have no special skill, take this time to try something new. Write a poem to praise the name of God. Try cooking a meal and then give it to a neighbor or provide it to a soup kitchen. Create a Christmas card by hand, with artwork and thoughtful text, and give it a friend, a neighbor, someone with whom you are at odds, or perhaps a complete stranger.

DAY 22

Give to God What You Are Able—
That Is Enough

I have much to be thankful for. I will tell you quite openly what the Lord has done for me. He has shown unto me the same mercy as unto King Solomon. All my desires have been satisfied; not only my desires of perfection, but even those of which I understood the vanity, in theory, if not in practice. I had always looked on Sister Agnes of Jesus as my model, and I wished to be like her in everything. She used to paint exquisite miniatures and write beautiful poems, and this inspired me with a desire to learn to paint, and express my thoughts in verse, that I might do some good to those around me. But I would not ask for these natural gifts, and my desire remained hidden in my heart.

THE STORY OF A SOUL, VIII, "PROFESSION OF SOEUR THÉRÈSE"

SCRIPTURE

He sat down opposite the treasury and observed how the crowd put money into the treasury. Many rich people put in large sums. A poor widow also came and put in two small coins worth a few cents. Calling his disciples to himself, he said to them, "Amen, I say to you, this poor widow put in more than all the other contributors to the treasury. For they have all contributed from their surplus wealth, but she, from her poverty, has contributed all she had, her whole livelihood."

MARK 12:41–44

PRAYER

Generous and loving God, you fill me with awe when I reflect on your great love, an unending ocean of charity and affection. I feel small when I consider my imperfections in my own ability to love. I feel as if there are limitations to my love and what I am able to give of myself to you. I am sometimes ashamed of how little I am able to give you, especially when I consider how much my friends and neighbors seem able and willing to give you. Grace me, Lord, with the courage and perseverance to give you all I can, and be merciful to me, dear Lord, a flawed being who is prone to make mistakes and fall far short of perfection. I know you love me for all that I am and I am grateful for your limitless mercy and compassion. Help me to love myself in that same way. Amen.

ADVENT ACTION

Spend ten to fifteen minutes in quiet reflection this evening or when you wake tomorrow morning. Consider the ways in which you've told the Lord you love him throughout the past week. Beyond the time you've spent at Mass or in formal prayer, how have you exhibited your love for God in your words, your actions toward friends and family, and your dealings with strangers? How have you praised the name of God in the little things you've done, in those actions that only you and God can see? In what ways have you fallen short of loving God the way you are called to? Consider these moments of weakness and offer them to God in prayer so that he might show you his mercy and forgiveness. Forgive yourself as well for these shortcomings. There is no need to empower the memory of your flaws once God has forgiven you. Follow his lead and forgive yourself.

DAY 23

Give to Those in Greatest Need and Do So Unconditionally

I ought to seek the companionship of those Sisters toward whom I feel a natural aversion, and try to be their good Samaritan. A word or a smile is often enough to put fresh life in a despondent soul. And yet it is not merely in the hope of giving consolation that I try to be kind. If it were, I know that I should soon be discouraged, for well-intentioned words are often totally misunderstood. Consequently, not to lose my time or labour, I try to act solely to please Our Lord, and follow this precept of the Gospel: "When thou makest a dinner or a supper, call not thy friends or thy brethren, lest perhaps they also invite thee again and a recompense be made to thee. But when thou makest a feast, call the poor, the maimed, the blind, and the lame, and thou shalt be blessed, because

they have naught wherewith to make thee recompense, and thy
Father Who seeth in secret will repay thee" (see Luke 14:12–14).

THE STORY OF A SOUL, X, "THE NEW COMMANDMENT"

SCRIPTURE

A man fell victim to robbers as he went down from Jerusalem to
Jericho. They stripped and beat him and went off leaving him
half-dead. A priest happened to be going down that road, but
when he saw him, he passed by on the opposite side. Likewise
a Levite came to the place, and when he saw him, he passed by
on the opposite side. But a Samaritan traveler who came upon
him was moved with compassion at the sight. He approached
the victim, poured oil and wine over his wounds and bandaged
them. Then he lifted him up on his own animal, took him to
an inn and cared for him. The next day he took out two silver
coins and gave them to the innkeeper with the instruction, "Take
care of him. If you spend more than what I have given you, I
shall repay you on my way back."

LUKE 10:30–35

PRAYER

God of unconditional and unsurpassed love, you loved me
into being and you have loved me throughout my life thus far.
Your love comes to me without strings attached, regardless of
the moments in my life when I choose a path that does not
align with your will. Grace me with the compassion to model
this love as my own. When people in my life do me wrong,

neglect me, or ignore me, help me to see past their action or inaction and love them regardless of their wrongdoing. Move my heart to love others—particularly those with whom I do not get along well—unconditionally, without strings attached. Allow me not to count the cost in giving to others, be it my spouse, my friend, my brother or sister, my parents, or someone I do not particularly like. Help me to love others for my own sake, for my own growth, and for the reward of knowing you at greater and greater depths. Amen.

ADVENT ACTION

Spend ten to fifteen minutes this evening or just after you wake tomorrow morning in quiet reflection. Allow a slideshow of sorts to run across your mind. Picture the faces of those people currently in your life who you—for reasons known or unknown—do not particularly like. Are these people worthy of the love of God? Of course they are. Are these people worthy of your love? That question may not be as easy to answer. Consider why it is so difficult—yet so important—to love those who are disagreeable to us. Consider the breakthrough you will make, in a spiritual sense, when you are able to love everyone beyond who you like and who you may not like. Soon you'll be able to love beyond these concepts of "like" and "dislike." Then you will be closer to the love of God than you could have possibly imagined before.

DAY 24

In the Face of Temptation, I Turn to Jesus

*E*ach time that my enemy would provoke me to combat, I behave as a gallant soldier. I know that a duel is an act of cowardice, and so, without once looking him in the face, I turn my back on the foe, then I hasten to my Saviour, and vow that I am ready to shed my blood in witness of my belief in Heaven....For what joy can be greater than to suffer for Thy Love? The more the suffering is and the less it appears before men, the more is it to Thy Honour and Glory. Even if—but I know it to be impossible—Thou shouldst not deign to heed my sufferings, I should still be happy to bear them, in the hope that by my tears I might perhaps prevent or atone for one sin against Faith.

THE STORY OF A SOUL, IX, "THE NIGHT OF THE SOUL"

SCRIPTURE

Owe nothing to anyone, except to love one another; for the one who loves another has fulfilled the law. The commandments, "You shall not commit adultery; you shall not kill; you shall not steal; you shall not covet," and whatever other commandment there may be, are summed up in this saying, (namely) "You shall love your neighbor as yourself." Love does no evil to the neighbor; hence, love is the fulfillment of the law. And do this because you know the time; it is the hour now for you to awake from sleep. For our salvation is nearer now than when we first believed; the night is advanced, the day is at hand. Let us then throw off the works of darkness (and) put on the armor of light; let us conduct ourselves properly as in the day...[.] But put on the Lord Jesus Christ, and make no provision for the desires of the flesh.

ROMANS 13:8–14

PRAYER

Father of mercy and compassion, oftentimes I feel as though I am beset at every turn by temptation. When I turn a corner there, confronting me, are myriad temptations: lust, greed, gluttony, sloth, envy, pride, and wrath. The last of these, when I encounter someone I do not like or who has done me wrong, is a powerful temptation. The desire for vengeance can be strong and, at the very least, my dislike for someone can freeze my heart to the love they need, the love I am called to extend from myself. Give me the strength to love, lest I fall into the temptation to harden my heart, and move me to follow the evil path placed before me by the dark one, the prince of lies. Open my heart to your love, loving God, and grace me with the fortitude and compassion that comes only from you. May I turn to you in this trial of temptation and may you move me to respond to my enemy with love. Amen.

ADVENT ACTION

Make it a point in the next twenty-four hours to allow the love of God for your enemies, or at the least someone you do not particularly care for, to shine through you. Allow the Lord to make you an instrument of his love, a beacon to those for whom you recoil or are tempted to ignore or, worse, willfully harm. Understand the power the temptation toward wrath can have over you, how it can affect your mood or your ability to love your neighbor—even that neighbor who has shown you no love. Turn to the Lord in prayer and ask for his strength.

This Advent action can be a difficult one. Recall how Jesus forgave those who crucified him. Shower the person(s) you dislike with acts of love—write them an encouraging note letting them know you are thinking of them (you don't have to tell them why!) during this Advent season. Leave a small gift on their doorstep (you might even do this anonymously). Praise them for some positive trait they bear, one that is God-given, one that allows them to shine the love of God into the world. Do this and see how the power of the temptation toward wrath dissipates in the face of love.

DAY 25

Our Gifts Are Not Our Own

Verily it is true that God alone can sound the heart. How short-sighted are His creatures! When they see a soul whose lights surpass their own, they conclude that the Divine Master loves them less. Since when has He lost the right to make use of one of His children, in order to supply the others with the nourishment they need? That right was not lost in the days of Pharaoh, for God said unto him: "And therefore have I raised thee, that I may show My power in thee, and My name may be spoken of throughout all the earth" (Exodus 9:16).

Generations have passed away since the Most High spoke these words, and His ways have not changed. He has ever chosen human instruments for the accomplishment of His work.

THE STORY OF A SOUL, X, "THE NEW COMMANDMENT"

SCRIPTURE

As each one has received a gift, use it to serve one another as good stewards of God's varied grace. Whoever preaches, let it be with the words of God; whoever serves, let it be with the strength that God supplies, so that in all things God may be glorified through Jesus Christ, to whom belong glory and dominion forever and ever. Amen.

1 PETER 4:10–11

PRAYER

Lord of generosity and wisdom, you have given each of us special and unique talents and skills through which we are called to praise your name and make your love known to the world around us. Guide us and grace us to always use these skills as you intended and not for our own selfish needs or for the purpose of harm. As your instruments of love, you love each of us in our own way, never neglecting our need nor denying our search for deeper union with you. Move me, loving Lord, to explore the depths of my person and better understand those unique gifts you have granted me according to your kindness and wisdom. Help me to discern the best use of those gifts and help me find creative ways to employ those precious gifts in praising your name and making your great love known to everyone I meet. Amen.

ADVENT ACTION

Spend ten to fifteen minutes in quiet reflection this evening or when you wake tomorrow morning. Consider the gifts God has given you, gifts unique to you. Ask yourself these questions and reflect upon them; allow God to guide your thoughts during this time: What is one specific gift the Lord has given to you that is unique to you? In what ways have you used this gift in the past to praise God's name and share his love? What are some fresh and creative paths you might take with this gift? Meditate on this question for as long as you like, welcoming the voice of God to speak to you throughout. How might this precious gift, placed within you by your loving Father, bring you closer to the Father of heaven? The Father gave us the gift of his Son. Explore the depths of your person and find your own gift; give it generously and with joy to your loving God.

DAY 26

Our Service to the Lord
Should Be Free From Worry

*Y*es, they will run—we shall all run together, for souls that are on fire can never be at rest. They may indeed, like St. Mary Magdalen, sit at the feet of Jesus, listening to His sweet and burning words, but, though they seem to give Him nothing, they give much more than Martha, who busied herself about many things. It is not Martha's work that Our Lord blames, but her over-solicitude [anxiety, worry]; His Blessed Mother humbly occupied herself in the same kind of work when she prepared the meals for the Holy Family. All the Saints have understood this, especially those who have illumined the earth with the light of Christ's teaching.

THE STORY OF A SOUL, XI, "A CANTICLE OF LOVE"

SCRIPTURE

As they continued their journey he entered a village where a woman whose name was Martha welcomed him. She had a sister named Mary (who) sat beside the Lord at his feet listening to him speak. Martha, burdened with much serving, came to him and said, "Lord, do you not care that my sister has left me by myself to do the serving? Tell her to help me." The Lord said to her in reply, "Martha, Martha, you are anxious and worried about many things. There is need of only one thing. Mary has chosen the better part and it will not be taken from her."

LUKE 10:38–42

PRAYER

Loving Father with gifts of grace, when I am in your presence and focused completely on you I am filled with peace and joy. When I am filled with your love there is no room for fear, for anxiety, or concern of any sort. I am untroubled and at ease. But when I keep any portion of my attention on matters other than you, I begin to sink into a sea of worry, just like St. Peter when he took his eyes away from your Son as that apostle walked across the water toward him. May I focus completely on you even in my work. Martha worried herself with matters that had nothing to do with your gifts of peace and comfort, and her example reminds me of what I am called to do in your presence, whether I am at work or in prayer. Grace me so that thoughts of worry do not enter my thoughts when I think on you. May my attention be on you alone and may I know only your peace and comfort. Amen.

ADVENT ACTION

When you are at work during the next few days—be it a full-time job, housework, gardening, or otherwise—make your work a matter of prayer and keep your focus completely on the Lord. This can take tremendous energy at first. Directing one's focus completely on the Lord and offering up one's work to him, without the distraction of outside worries or myriad random thoughts entering the mind, can be a trying task—and not feel like prayer at all. The key is to remind yourself that this is indeed prayer, communication with the Lord in the truest sense. This is the act of your work guided by the love of God. This is a conversation between you and God through your work. This is a sanctification of your work by the Lord as it is offered to him in praise of his name. Keep your focus on the Lord during your work these next few days. See how this focus transforms your work and reduces any worry that was previously attached to it.

DAY 27

The Bread of Life Is Given to Us Who Make a Place for Him

I shall always remember my First Communion Day as one of unclouded happiness. It seems to me that I could not have been better prepared. Do you remember, dear Mother, the charming little book you gave me three months before the great day? I found in it a helpful method which prepared me gradually and thoroughly. It is true I had been thinking about my First Communion for a long time, but, as your precious manuscript told me, I must stir up in my heart fresh transports of love and fill it anew with flowers. So, each day I made a number of little sacrifices and acts of love, which were to be changed into so many flowers: now violets, another time roses, then cornflowers, daisies, or forget-me-nots—in a word, all nature's blossoms were to form in me a cradle for the Holy Child.

THE STORY OF A SOUL, IV, "FIRST COMMUNION AND CONFIRMATION"

SCRIPTURE

[Jesus said,] "This is my body that is for you. Do this in remembrance of me." In the same way also the cup, after supper, saying, "This cup is the new covenant in my blood. Do this, as often as you drink it, in remembrance of me." For as often as you eat this bread and drink the cup, you proclaim the death of the Lord until he comes.

1 CORINTHIANS 11:24–26

So Jesus said to them, "Amen, amen, I say to you, it was not Moses who gave the bread from heaven; my Father gives you the true bread from heaven. For the bread of God is that which comes down from heaven and gives life to the world."

JOHN 6:32–33

PRAYER

Generous and loving Lord, you who humbly grant us your immense grace in the sacrament of the holy Eucharist, we praise your name for every gift you give us. Through the Eucharist, we are united with you, your flesh transforms our own, and we are sanctified by your Body and Blood. May your name be forever praised, loving God, for the gift of your Son and for his victory over death. By your grace and loving hand, we will be brought to eternal life by your side to share in your love forever and always. Move me to share your love with everyone I encounter throughout my day, and may the holy Communion we share at Mass unite me with your love and, transformed by that love, may I praise your name without hesitation and without fear, for you are my rock and my loving shepherd. I ask all of this in praise of your merciful and compassionate heart and in the name of your Son, our Lord Jesus Christ. Amen.

ADVENT ACTION

The next time you receive the Eucharist, spend the brief period that follows in quiet contemplation. (It is quite likely that this is a practice you currently incorporate at this time during the Mass.) Consider during this time how you are transformed by the Body and Blood of your Lord Jesus Christ. How does the union of his flesh with your own move you to love your neighbor as the Lord God loves you? How does the Eucharist move you to praise the name of God in your words and actions? How does it transform your relationship with the members of your family? Of your parish? Those with whom you work? The strangers—young and old, rich and poor, black and white— you encounter throughout the coming day and week? Are you moved, following the reception of holy Communion—to serve as an instrument of the Lord, allowing his grace to open your heart to the love he desires to shine upon the world through you as his instrument?

DAY 28

The Communion of Saints
Inspires the Uncertain Mind

J was now fourteen and a half, and in six months' time the blessed feast of Christmas would be here. I had resolved to enter the Carmel at the same hour at which a year before I had received the grace of conversion.

I chose the feast of Pentecost on which to make my great disclosure. All day I was praying for light from the Holy Ghost, and begging the Apostles to pray for me, to inspire me with the words I ought to use. Were they not the very ones to help a timid child whom God destines to become an apostle of apostles by prayer and sacrifice?

THE STORY OF A SOUL, V, "VOCATION OF THÉRÈSE"

SCRIPTURE

*What was from the beginning, what we have heard, what we
have seen with our eyes, what we looked upon and touched
with our hands concerns the word of life—for the life was made
visible; we have seen it and testify to it and proclaim to you the
eternal life that was with the Father and was made visible to
us—what we have seen and heard we proclaim now to you, so
that you too may have fellowship with us; for our fellowship is
with the Father and with his Son, Jesus Christ. We are writing
this so that our joy may be complete.*

*Now this is the message that we have heard from him and
proclaim to you: God is light, and in him there is no darkness at
all. If we say, "We have fellowship with him," while we continue
to walk in darkness, we lie and do not act in truth. But if we walk
in the light as he is in the light, then we have fellowship with one
another, and the blood of his Son Jesus cleanses us from all sin.*

1 JOHN 1:1–7

PRAYER

Merciful Father and God of compassion, you who provides
for us on our journey to you, you equip us with the graces
we need to follow your word, and among these graces is our
recourse to the communion of saints. Those blessed and
beloved souls at your side intercede on our behalf when we
call upon their names in times of need. Each of the holy men
and women were graced with special gifts during their time
upon this earth and, after they have passed into eternal life,

continue to share these gifts with those of us who call out for guidance in accord with their specific virtues. Guide me, oh Lord, to call upon these beautiful saints as I seek to stay upon the path to your eternal home. Open my heart to the lessons they can teach me about their own struggles, sacrifices, and periods of peace and joy when they walked upon this earth as I do now. Bend you ear, loving Father, and give heed to their words as they intercede on my behalf. They seek for me what they have found in your heavenly home. Amen.

ADVENT ACTION

In what ways have you fostered your relationship with the communion of saints? Is there a special saint to whom you call out to in times of need? When you are suffering during periods of sadness or depression? When you've lost something dear to you? When an expectant mother you know is in the midst of a particularly difficult pregnancy? Consider locating a book on the saints or searching the Internet for a site that informs you to whom you can appeal in any case and for any area of support. Converse with this saint in prayer, open your heart to what concerns you and ask that this saint intercede for you, offering your prayer as his or her own in requesting the special grace from God needed to address the given situation with the love and grace it requires. Understand that the saint to whom you pray is a conduit to the Father, a channel through which your prayer to the Lord reaches him in a special way, through a saint who has a unique connection to the matter at hand.

PART II

~

READINGS
for the
TWELVE DAYS
of
CHRISTMAS

DAY 1

God Loves Us Deeply, Even in Times of Weakness

*I*n truth I am no Saint, as this frame of mind well shows. I ought not to rejoice in my dryness of soul, but rather attribute it to my want of fervour and fidelity. That I fall asleep so often during meditation, and thanksgiving after Communion, should distress me. Well, I am not distressed. I reflect that little children are equally dear to their parents whether they are asleep or awake; that, in order to perform operations, doctors put their patients to sleep; and finally that "the Lord knoweth our frame, He remembereth that we are but dust" (Psalm 102 [103]:14).

THE STORY OF A SOUL, VIII, "PROFESSION OF SOEUR THÉRÈSE"

SCRIPTURE

[He] said to me, "My grace is sufficient for you, for power is made perfect in weakness." I will rather boast most gladly of my weaknesses, in order that the power of Christ may dwell with me. Therefore, I am content with weaknesses, insults, hardships, persecutions, and constraints, for the sake of Christ; for when I am weak, then I am strong.

2 CORINTHIANS 12:9–10

Peter (said) to them, "Repent and be baptized, every one of you, in the name of Jesus Christ for the forgiveness of your sins; and you will receive the gift of the holy Spirit...."

ACTS 2:38

PRAYER

Father of mercy and abiding love, you know well our human weakness. You know we fall short many times throughout our lives; we fail to live up to our promise of fidelity to your word, and we fail ourselves in staying true to your path and knowing your peace and graces. Instead of desiring that we give in to feelings of deep guilt and sadness, you ask that we open our hearts to you and ask for your forgiveness, for you want only for us to be united to you. Your love is so strong and desire for us so great, that you overcome our frailty and grace us with the wisdom and hope to rely on your strength and guidance. What we can accomplish in this world is nothing without your loving hand guiding us in your ways, according to the word you have given us to know you and your peace to the greatest depths. Amen.

ADVENT ACTION

During this season of Christmas, consider the ways in which you can approach God in a special way and reflect on ways you can open your heart to his grace so that he might draw you closer to the myriad graces he provides. God understands our weakness, our human frailty. He experienced our humanity in every way when he walked among us 2,000 years ago; he knows what we are capable of, he knows that just as there are times when we are strong in our faith and stay true to his path, there are also those times when we stray from his word and are in need of his guiding hand. Make it a point to participate in the sacrament of reconciliation during the coming week and open you heart, in all its weakness and with all its yearning, to be united fully with the Lord.

DAY 2

All Is Well When You Seek the Will of God

*A*ll those beloved by God have followed the inspiration of the Holy Ghost, who commanded the prophets to write: "Tell the just man that all is well" (see Isaiah: 3:10). Yes, all is well when one seeks only the Master's Will....

You know it has ever been my desire to become a Saint, but I have always felt, in comparing myself with the Saints, that I am as far removed from them as the grain of sand, which the passer-by tramples underfoot, is remote from the mountain whose summit is lost in the clouds.

THE STORY OF A SOUL, IX, "THE NIGHT OF THE SOUL"

SCRIPTURE

[T]hose who live according to the flesh are concerned with the things of the flesh, but those who live according to the spirit with the things of the spirit. The concern of the flesh is death, but the concern of the spirit is life and peace. For the concern of the flesh is hostility toward God; it does not submit to the law of God, nor can it; and those who are in the flesh cannot please God.

But you are not in the flesh; on the contrary, you are in the spirit, if only the Spirit of God dwells in you. Whoever does not have the Spirit of Christ does not belong to him. But if Christ is in you, although the body is dead because of sin, the spirit is alive because of righteousness. If the Spirit of the one who raised Jesus from the dead dwells in you, the one who raised Christ from the dead will give life to your mortal bodies also, through his Spirit that dwells in you.

ROMANS 8:5–11

PRAYER

Father of grace and guidance, when I seek to do your will I know only happiness and I enjoy the peace your company affords. You have graced humanity with the ability to choose you or to choose to follow paths contrary to your will. The saints in heaven enjoy your love for all eternity; I desire this reality as well, even though I sometimes stray from your path because of my human frailty. By your grace and guidance I know I will be united for all eternity with you, in the company of your saints, in the blessed joy that is your heavenly kingdom. Grace me with the perseverance to seek only you in everything I say, everything I do, and in my interaction with all I encounter throughout my days. By choosing you and directing my will so that I stay upon the path of virtue, I will know only happiness and enjoy the peace your company affords. Amen.

ADVENT ACTION

Temperance is one of the four cardinal virtues of the Catholic Church. This virtue centers on one's ability to moderate the earthly pleasures of our human existence. Temperance is the capacity to enjoy one's temporal existence in a manner of discretion so that his appetites do not control his life in an unhealthy fashion.

Spend ten to fifteen minutes in quiet reflection this evening or when you wake tomorrow morning. Consider the ways in which you enjoy the pleasures of this world that—when taken in moderation—contribute to and enhance the life you lead as a creation of God's love. In what ways do these experiences bring you closer to your heavenly Father? In what ways—when the virtue of temperance is absent—can these pleasures control the will and move the appetite in the direction of temptation and sin? Pray for the grace of God that you may always be temperate in your discretion.

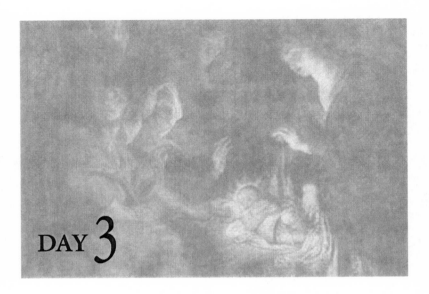

DAY 3

God Is the Painter, I Am His Brush

*I*f an artist's canvas could but think and speak, surely it would never complain of being touched and re-touched by the brush, nor would it feel envious thereof, knowing that all its beauty is due to the artist alone. So, too, the brush itself could not boast of the masterpiece it had helped to produce, for it must know that an artist is never at a loss; that difficulties do but stimulate him; and that at times it pleases him to make use of instruments the most unlikely and defective.

THE STORY OF A SOUL, X, "THE NEW COMMANDMENT"

SCRIPTURE

In the beginning, when God created the heavens and the earth
— and the earth was without form or shape, with darkness
over the abyss and a mighty wind sweeping over the waters.
Then God said: Let there be light, and there was light. God saw
that the light was good. God then separated the light from the
darkness. God called the light "day," and the darkness he called
"night." Evening came, and morning followed—the first day.

Then God said: Let there be a dome in the middle of the
waters, to separate one body of water from the other. God made
the dome, and it separated the water below the dome from the
water above the dome. And so it happened. God called the dome
"sky." Evening came, and morning followed—the second day.

Then God said: Let the water under the sky be gathered
into a single basin, so that the dry land may appear. And so it
happened: the water under the sky was gathered into its basin,
and the dry land appeared. God called the dry land "earth," and
the basin of water he called "sea." God saw that it was good.

GENESIS 1:1–10

PRAYER

God of greatness and creator of all that is beautiful, grace
me with the cardinal virtue of fortitude, that I might be firm
and resolute in the face of temptation. Move me to see your
goodness in all things and stir my heart that I seek only this
goodness throughout my days upon this earth. Grace me with
unwavering faith and help me to conquer fear and be coura-

geous in the face of persecution. May I serve you and only you, even to death should I be asked to give my life for love of you. You are the painter and I am your brush. Color the world with your love and use me as your instrument. Work through me so I might shine your love upon the world and make known your holy name to all who cross my path. I ask this in the name of your Son, our Lord Jesus Christ. Amen.

ADVENT ACTION

Spend ten to fifteen minutes in quiet reflection this evening or when you wake tomorrow morning. Reflect upon the meaning of the word "epiphany." In a general sense, the word means "an appearance or manifestation especially of a divine being." Of course, as Christians, we generally understand the meaning of the word in a more specific sense: the Epiphany is the Christian feast celebrating the manifestation of the divine nature of Jesus to the Gentiles as represented by the wise men.

In what ways are God and his love made manifest to you in your daily life? How about a hug or a kiss from a loved one? His love is also made known through special events like a baptism, a wedding, in the bread and wine (transformed into the Body and Blood of Christ) in the sacrament of the Eucharist. Reflect upon other concrete ways you experience God in your life. In what ways can you serve as God's brush, aiding our Lord in painting the beauty of his love upon the earth so his name and his comfort is known to all? Pray to the Lord that he grace you with the fortitude to be strong in the midst of temptation so you can represent his love to others without any stain of sin.

DAY 4

The Lord Is Just, Fear Nothing

*O*ur Lord has granted me the grace never to fear the conflict; at all costs I must do my duty. I have more than once been told: "If you want me to obey, you must be gentle and not severe, otherwise you will gain nothing." But no one is a good judge in his own case. During a painful operation a child will be sure to cry out and say that the remedy is worse than the disease; but if after a few days he is cured, then he is greatly delighted that he can run about and play. And it is the same with souls: they soon recognize that a little bitter is better than too much sweet, and they are not afraid to make the acknowledgment. Sometimes the change which takes place from one day to another seems almost magical.

THE STORY OF A SOUL, X, "THE NEW COMMANDMENT"

You have heard that it was said, "An eye for an eye and a tooth for a tooth." But I say to you, offer no resistance to one who is evil. When someone strikes you on (your) right cheek, turn the other one to him as well.

MATTHEW 5:38–39

Thus says the LORD: "Observe what is right, do what is just; for my salvation is about to come, my justice, about to be revealed."

ISAIAH 56:1

When justice is done it is a joy for the just, downfall for evildoers.

PROVERBS 21:15

PRAYER

God of justice, grace me with the cardinal virtue to practice justice in my own life. May I be just in my dealings with everyone I encounter throughout my day. May I treat others with the respect they deserve, even on the occasions when they do me wrong. May I see the face of your Son, Jesus, when I look into the face of another. May I respond with love to evil. May the justice I practice be the justice of love, and may I praise and respect your name as I treat with respect my fellow brother and sisters. May my practice of justice become a habit so that my left hand knows not what my right is doing. May my practice of justice be such that I respond with love to everyone I meet without even a consideration to an action contrary to love. I ask all of this in the name of your Son, our Lord Jesus Christ. Amen.

ADVENT ACTION

Justice is another of the four "cardinal" virtues of the Catholic Church. This virtue centers on one's ability to respect the rights of all humanity, conduct one's relationships with an eye toward harmony, and value the common good. A just person practices right thinking and a standard of conduct toward one's neighbor that reflects the love of God for all people.

Spend ten to fifteen minutes in quiet reflection this evening or when you wake tomorrow morning. Consider the ways in which you practice justice toward your fellow brothers and sisters. How do you respond to others in the face of acts of injustice they perpetrate against you? Do you respond in love? Do you "turn the other cheek?" In what ways do you promote harmony and the common good in your community? Spend a few minutes in prayer asking God to strengthen you in the virtue of justice. Ask him to grace you with the strength to act justly on all occasions.

DAY 5

The Lord Welcomes Our Conversation With Him

I see so many beautiful horizons, such infinitely varied tints, that the palette of the Divine Painter will alone, after the darkness of this life, be able to supply me with the colours wherewith I may portray the wonders that my soul descries [meaning: discovers by careful observation]. Since, however, you have expressed a desire to penetrate into the hidden sanctuary of my heart, and to have in writing what was the most consoling dream of my life, I will end this story of my soul, by an act of obedience. If you will allow me, it is to Jesus I will address myself, for in this way I shall speak more easily. You may find my expressions somewhat exaggerated, but I assure you there is no exaggeration in my heart—there all is calm and peace.

THE STORY OF A SOUL, XI, "A CANTICLE OF LOVE"

SCRIPTURE

Ask and it will be given to you; seek and you will find; knock and the door will be opened to you. For everyone who asks, receives; and the one who seeks, finds; and to the one who knocks, the door will be opened.

MATTHEW 7:7–8

But if any of you lacks wisdom, he should ask God who gives to all generously and ungrudgingly, and he will be given it. But he should ask in faith, not doubting, for the one who doubts is like a wave of the sea that is driven and tossed about by the wind. For that person must not suppose that he will receive anything from the Lord, since he is a man of two minds, unstable in all his ways.

JAMES 1:5–8

PRAYER

God of love, you welcome our dialogue with you. Just as our Lord Jesus Christ conversed easily with those he encountered during his time on earth among us, he welcomes our questions, our requests, and our simple welcome that he occupy the innermost corners of our hearts. I praise your holy name, oh Lord, for you are the one who calls us to draw ever nearer to your loving heart and you are the one who graces us with the courage and perseverance to seek you out despite the temptations and myriad threats that surround us. Grace us with the desire to seek the true good in all circumstances and grant me the courage to pursue it with every ounce of my being. May I act according to the virtue of prudence so that my conscience forever guides me to your loving heart. Amen.

ADVENT ACTION

Prudence is another of the four cardinal virtues of the Catholic Church. This virtue guides the others virtues and centers on one's ability—through the grace and guidance of God—to discern the real good in all situations and pursue what is right, achieving goodness through the judgment of one's conscience.

Spend ten to fifteen minutes in quiet reflection this evening or when you wake tomorrow morning. Consider the ways in which the virtue of prudence guides your life. In what specific instances over the past few weeks have you employed the God-given ability to reason when faced with matters of good and evil? How does the virtue of prudence help you to find the good in all things? How does this virtue assist when you encounter difficult or irritating people? Spend a few minutes in prayer asking God to strengthen you in the virtue of prudence. Ask him to grace you with the strength to recognize his presence in all things and—where there is temptation—ask that he keep you from sin.

DAY 6

The Devil Fears the Lord's Faithful Servant

I remember a dream I had at that age which impressed itself very deeply on my memory. I thought I was walking alone in the garden when, suddenly, I saw…two hideous little devils dancing with surprising agility on a barrel of lime, in spite of the heavy irons attached to their feet. At first they cast fiery glances at me; then, as though suddenly terrified, I saw them, in the twinkling of an eye, throw themselves down to the bottom of the barrel, from which they came out somehow, only to run and hide themselves in the laundry which opened into the garden. Finding them such cowards, I wanted to know what they were going to do, and, overcoming my fears, I went to the window…. From time to time they came nearer, peering through the windows with an uneasy air, then, seeing that I was still there, they began to run about again looking quite desperate.

Of course this dream was nothing extraordinary; yet I think Our Lord made use of it to show me that a soul in the state of grace has nothing to fear from the devil, who is a coward, and will even fly from the gaze of a little child.

THE STORY OF A SOUL, I, "EARLIEST MEMORIES"

SCRIPTURE

Everyone who has this hope based on [the Father] makes himself pure, as he is pure. Everyone who commits sin commits lawlessness, for sin is lawlessness. You know that he was revealed to take away sins, and in him there is no sin. No one who remains in him sins; no one who sins has seen him or known him. Children, let no one deceive you. The person who acts in righteousness is righteous, just as he is righteous. Whoever sins belongs to the devil, because the devil has sinned from the beginning. Indeed, the Son of God was revealed to destroy the works of the devil. No one who is begotten by God commits sin, because God's seed remains in him; he cannot sin because he is begotten by God. In this way, the children of God and the children of the devil are made plain; no one who fails to act in righteousness belongs to God, nor anyone who does not love his brother.

1 JOHN 3:3–10

PRAYER

Father of protection and guidance, you are the one who keeps us from the temptations of the devil. We trust our safety to your strength and the cowardly devil runs away in fear. The devil is a weak and craven creature, deplorable in every way. He relies on our weakness and upon the occasions when we stumble and lose our way along the Father's path of righteousness. But when we call upon the Father's grace and rely on his strength, the devil is left with nothing but his own fear. The devil runs in the face of a soul in the state of grace. The devil delights in our sin but our Lord rescues us time and again, ever loyal to his beloved sons and daughters of the earth. For this fidelity, for this enduring strength and protection we praise his holy name in our words and our deeds. Amen.

ADVENT ACTION

Spend ten to fifteen minutes in quiet reflection this evening or when you wake tomorrow morning. Consider the strength and protection the Father provides you. Consider the grace he gives unconditionally and without reserve. In this state of reflection, offer a prayer of praise to the Father in your own words. Give him thanks for the guidance he gives you throughout your day. Call to mind those times in the past week when you were tempted from the path of goodness with thoughts of vengeance, jealousy, wrath, lust, and so on. Did you call upon the Father during these times of temptation, when your weaknesses were exploited by the lies of the devil? If you asked for his grace, how did his strength move you to persevere in righteousness in the face of this temptation? Consider the goodness of the Father throughout your life. Know that you can rely on his guiding hand in every way and at every moment.

DAY 7

God Dwells in the Midst of a Loving Family

*S*oon after my Mother's death, Papa made up his mind to leave Alençon and live at Lisieux, so that we might be near our uncle, my Mother's brother. He made this sacrifice in order that my young sisters should have the benefit of their aunt's guidance in their new life, and that she might act as a mother toward them. I did not feel any grief at leaving my native town: children love change and anything out of the common, and so I was pleased to come to Lisieux. I remember the journey quite well, and our arrival in the evening at my uncle's house, and I can still see my little cousins, Jeanne and Marie, waiting on the doorstep with my aunt. How touching was the affection all these dear ones showed us!

THE STORY OF A SOUL, II, "A CATHOLIC HOUSEHOLD"

SCRIPTURE

Again, I say to you, if two of you agree on earth about anything for which they are to pray, it shall be granted to them by my heavenly Father. For where two or three are gathered together in my name, there am I in the midst of them.

MATTHEW 18:19–20

Your wife will be like a fruitful vine
within your home,
Your children like young olive plants
around your table.

PSALM 128:3

PRAYER

Triune God—Father, Son, and Holy Spirit, though you are three distinct persons, you are one God. In a similar manner and on a much smaller scale, our families consist of multiple persons, but we exist as a single unit, ideally rooted in the model of love you share as the Holy Trinity. Grace us, dear Lord, with the ability to appreciate our family members. Help us to accept who they are, warts and all. Move us to show these people acts of kindness, of compassion, of understanding. In the Holy Family we see a nurturing mother, a son growing in wisdom, and a father figure who provides for his family. Each one supports the others in the way the heavenly Father intended for families throughout the world and throughout history. May you continue to guide us in the ways of love, dear Father, and strengthen our familial bond through the generous love you give to us as a model of the love we are called to share with the members of our family. Amen.

ADVENT ACTION

Sometime today or tomorrow, take ten to fifteen minutes and compose a handwritten note (or an email) to a member of your family, perhaps someone with whom you have clashed during the course of your relationship with one another. Express the ways in which you value family and the ways in which family members can support and encourage one another. In a spirit of reconciliation, express your gratitude for this person and the times when he or she helped or supported you in some specific manner. Tell this person that even though the two of you have had your differences, you appreciate his or her presence in your life. Let him or her know that you pray for his or her well-being and ask the individual to pray for you as well, that you might be strong in your faith and live your life as a willing servant of God, expressing his love for everyone but most of all for your family members.

DAY 8

With Faith, Even the Littlest of Us Are Raised Up

When a gardener gives special attention to a fruit which he wishes to ripen early, he does so, not with a view to leaving it on the tree, but in order to place it on a well-spread table. Our Lord lavished His favours on His Little Flower in the same way. He wishes His Mercies to shine forth in me—He Who, while on earth, cried out in a transport of joy: "I bless Thee, O Father, because Thou hast hidden these things from the wise and prudent and hast revealed them to little ones" (see Luke 19:26).

THE STORY OF A SOUL, V, "VOCATION OF THÉRÈSE"

SCRIPTURE

Amen, I say to you, if you have faith the size of a mustard seed, you will say to this mountain, "Move from here to there," and it will move. Nothing will be impossible for you.

MATTHEW 17:20

[W]ithout faith it is impossible to please him, for anyone who approaches God must believe that he exists and that he rewards those who seek him.

HEBREWS 11:6

PRAYER

God of infinite power and tender mercy, you make yourself known to us in every corner of our lives, revealing your love for us in the people we meet, nourishing our bodies with food and drink, and refreshing our energy with the peace of sleep. Our faith in you is rewarded with love and we strengthen this bond all the more with works of love in praise of your name and in service to your beloved humanity as your instrument of compassion and blessing to all those we encounter during our days. Grace my heart, dear Lord, soften it so that I might allow your love to flow through me and into the hearts others, showering your love upon them as a conduit to the peace that one can experience when you are made known. I ask this in the name of your Son, our Lord Jesus Christ. Amen.

ADVENT ACTION

Sometime within the next week, make it a point to contact an acquaintance, someone you know but who you do not know all that well. Let this person know that you have been praying for her, praying that the Lord will shower her with graces throughout the New Year. Ask her if there is anything specific for which she would like you to pray. Is there a person in her life who is struggling with some issue? Is there a person close to her who is suffering from a long-running illness? Would the support of your prayers benefit her as she deals with some specific stressor at home or at work? This person does not need to be specific in her need for prayerful support. Just a general idea of the strength and encouragement she is seeking from the Lord is enough to point your prayers in the right direction. The support you offer is a splendid way to let this person know that God is looking out for her (even though she might feel insignificant and unworthy of his love) and moving you to serve as an instrument of his love.

DAY 9

May I Give Myself Without Distraction to the Lord

Now I have no desire left, unless it be to love Jesus even unto folly! It is Love alone that draws me. I no longer wish either for suffering or death, yet both are precious to me. Long did I call upon them as the messengers of joy. I have suffered much....From earliest childhood I have imagined that the Little Flower would be gathered in its springtime; now, the spirit of self-abandonment alone is my guide. I have no other compass, and know not how to ask anything with eagerness, save the perfect accomplishment of God's designs upon my soul. I can say these words of the Canticle of our Father, St. John of the Cross:

"I drank deep in the cellar of my Friend, and, coming forth again, knew naught of all this plain, and lost the flock I erst was wont to tend. My soul and all its wealth I gave to be His Own; no more I tend my flock, all other work is done, and all my exercise is Love alone" (Spiritual Canticle: Stanzas 18 and 20).

THE STORY OF A SOUL, VIII, "PROFESSION OF SOEUR THÉRÈSE"

SCRIPTURE

I urge you therefore, brothers, by the mercies of God, to offer your bodies as a living sacrifice, holy and pleasing to God, your spiritual worship. Do not conform yourselves to this age but be transformed by the renewal of your mind, that you may discern what is the will of God, what is good and pleasing and perfect. For by the grace given to me I tell everyone among you not to think of himself more highly than one ought to think, but to think soberly, each according to the measure of faith that God has apportioned.

ROMANS 12:1–3

PRAYER

God of love, throughout my days I am confronted by temptations that present themselves as something greater and more desirable than you. These distractions often cause me worry because, when I am fooled into relying upon them, I become anxious that I might lose them or that someone will come and take them away from me. It is you who rescues me from this foolishness, dear Lord. I can never lose you and no one can take you away from me. Help me, good and generous God, to seek only you and focus my mind and heart on you and you alone. Keep me from all temptations and draw me ever closer to your side. Your gift is your Son, and this gift is all I need. May my faith in Christ Jesus light the way to his side and to the eternal peace he offers to me in loving friendship. Amen.

ADVENT ACTION

Spend ten to fifteen minutes in quiet reflection this evening or when you wake tomorrow morning. Consider the distractions that confronted you over the past day or two. What did you choose instead of God? Why did you choose these lesser goods? In what ways do these distractions keep you from experiencing the love and grace of God? In what ways do these distractions harm your relationships with family and friends? After you have reflected on these questions, spend five minutes in conversation with God. Ask him for the grace to keep your mind, body, and heart focused on his love. Ask him to intervene with his grace during those times throughout your day when you are confronted by the distraction of temptation. Ask for the grace to see God's presence at work in every facet of your life so that distractions have no place to take root and draw your focus from the love of God.

DAY 10

Find the Lord in the Quiet Corners of Your Life

*S*oon after my First Communion I went into retreat again, before being confirmed. I prepared myself with the greatest care for the coming of the Holy Ghost; I could not understand anyone not doing so before receiving this Sacrament of Love. As the ceremony could not take place on the day fixed, I had the consolation of remaining somewhat longer in retreat. How happy I felt! Like the Apostles, I looked with joy for the promised Comforter, gladdened by the thought that I should soon be a perfect Christian, and have the holy Cross, the symbol of this wondrous Sacrament, traced upon my forehead for eternity. I did not feel the mighty wind of the first Pentecost, but rather the gentle breeze which the prophet Elias heard on Mount Horeb. On that day I received the gift of fortitude in suffering—a gift I needed sorely, for the martyrdom of my soul was soon to begin.

THE STORY OF A SOUL, IV, "FIRST COMMUNION AND CONFIRMATION"

SCRIPTURE

Then the LORD said: "Go out and stand on the mountain before the LORD; the LORD will pass by."

There was a strong and violent wind rending the mountains and crushing rocks before the LORD—but the LORD was not in the wind; after the wind, an earthquake—but the LORD was not in the earthquake; after the earthquake, fire—but the LORD was not in the fire; after the fire, a light silent sound.

When he heard this, Elijah hid his face in his cloak and went out and stood at the entrance of the cave. A voice said to him, Why are you here, Elijah? He replied, "I have been most zealous for the LORD, the God of hosts, but the Israelites have forsaken your covenant. They have destroyed your altars and murdered your prophets by the sword. I alone remain, and they seek to take my life."

1 KINGS 19:11–14

PRAYER

Merciful and generous Father, you seek to fill every area of my life with your love. You grace me with the perseverance to seek you and find you in everything I do and in everyone I meet. Lord, just as I am able to see the smallest flower growing in a dry and dirty patch of desert earth, so am I able to see the flower of your love abloom in the most desperate situations. There are moments of spiritual dryness during my life, dear Lord, when it seems you are nowhere to be seen. I have found that during these times, when I look hard enough and focus all of my attention on finding you, I am able to see you where I once thought you were absent. Even in the face of hatred and evil, I know that you are present, loving Father. With you as my rock, as my guiding hand, I fear nothing for I know I am protected by your love and kept safe forever by your side. Amen.

ADVENT ACTION

Spend ten to fifteen minutes in quiet reflection this evening or when you wake tomorrow morning. Consider the numerous ways that God has made himself present to you over the last twenty-four to forty-eight hours. How has he spoken to you through your friends, your family, and the many people you have encountered during the past day or two? Which of these encounters have been especially encouraging and comforting? Have some of these encounters been difficult and challenging? In what ways did you experience the hand of God at work during these occasions? Did these experiences strengthen or challenge your relationship with God? What recent, specific challenges in your life have affected your relationship with God? Do you view these challenging times as an opportunity to strengthen your relationship with God?

DAY 11

Make My Soul a Fitting Place for Jesus to Make His Home

I picture my soul as a piece of waste ground and beg Our Blessed Lady to take away my imperfections—which are as heaps of rubbish—and to build upon it a splendid tabernacle worthy of Heaven, and adorn it with her own adornments. Then I invite all the Angels and Saints to come and sing canticles of love, and it seems to me that Jesus is well pleased to see Himself received so grandly, and I share in His joy. But all this does not prevent distractions and drowsiness from troubling me, and not infrequently I resolve to continue my thanksgiving throughout the day....You see, dear Mother, that my way is not the way of fear; I can always make myself happy, and profit by my imperfections, and Our Lord Himself encourages me in this path.

THE STORY OF A SOUL, VIII, "PROFESSION OF SOEUR THÉRÈSE"

SCRIPTURE

The one who supplies seed to the sower and bread for food will supply and multiply your seed and increase the harvest of your righteousness. You are being enriched in every way for all generosity, which through us produces thanksgiving to God.... Through the evidence of this service, you are glorifying God for your obedient confession of the gospel of Christ and the generosity of your contribution to them and to all others, while in prayer on your behalf they long for you, because of the surpassing grace of God upon you. Thanks be to God for his indescribable gift!

2 CORINTHIANS 9:10–11, 13–15

PRAYER

Generous and loving God, through your word I am made generous in my own right. You have grown within me a heart of compassionate love, one that is driven to praise your name by the love I sow throughout the world, in my encounters with others and in the charitable acts I am moved to perform by your guiding hand. It is you who has opened in my heart a place where the word can take root, make his home, and grow within me an abundance of love that will shine for all to see. It is only through you and your generosity that I am able to serve as your instrument. You soften my heart, you move me to call upon the Blessed Virgin and the angels and saints so that I might be fortified with the courage and perseverance to praise your name in the face of any and all temptation. For all of this and more I praise your name. Amen.

ADVENT ACTION

As you approach the conclusion of these days of Advent and Christmas with St. Thérèse, spend ten to fifteen minutes in quiet reflection this evening or when you wake tomorrow morning. Consider the following: What are those blessings in my life for which I am truly grateful? Family? Friends? Good health? A loving spouse? Beautiful children and/or grandchildren? A job in which I take pleasure? Hobbies that refresh me and serve as a blessing to others and/or to praise the name of God?

Pray, asking God to grace you with focus and gratitude on all that he has given you, especially when you catch yourself dwelling on those things that you do not have and directing your attention to feelings of jealousy or self-pity. Focus your mind and heart on what you *do* have and explore the ways in which you can love God and your neighbor to even greater depths through the graces the Lord has bestowed upon you.

DAY 12

The Lord Gives Me Beautiful Flowers in Abundance

*T*alking of my desires, I must tell you about others of quite a different kind, which the Divine Master has also been pleased to grant: childish desires....You know, dear Mother, how fond I am of flowers. When I made myself a prisoner at the age of fifteen, I gave up for ever the delights of rambling through meadows bright with the treasures of spring. Well, I never possessed so many flowers as I have had since entering the Carmel. In the world young men present their betrothed with beautiful bouquets, and Jesus did not forget me. For His Altar I received, in abundance, all the flowers I loved best: cornflowers, poppies, marguerites—one little friend only was missing, the purple vetch. I longed to see it again, and at last it came to gladden me and show that, in the least as in the greatest, God gives a hundred-fold, even in this life, to those who have left all for His Love.

THE STORY OF A SOUL, VIII, "PROFESSION OF SOEUR THÉRÈSE"

SCRIPTURE

Do not be deceived...all good giving and every perfect gift is from above, coming down from the Father of lights, with whom there is no alteration or shadow caused by change. He willed to give us birth by the word of truth that we may be a kind of firstfruits of his creatures. Know this, my dear brothers: everyone should be quick to hear, slow to speak, slow to wrath, for the wrath of a man does not accomplish the righteousness of God. Therefore, put away all filth and evil excess and humbly welcome the word that has been planted in you and is able to save your souls. Be doers of the word and not hearers only....

JAMES 1:16–22

PRAYER

Generous and merciful Father, you give me every good thing, you protect me from temptation, you are my rock and my shield, you shower my life with graces and gifts beyond all expectation, beyond my imagination. May I remain forever at your side, both here on earth and into the afterlife. By the guiding and nourishing Word you have given as your greatest gift, your only Son given to us on Christmas Day, we find every portion of our humanity sanctified by grace and mercy. Christmas Day eventually leads us to the final glory of Easter, when the separation between God and humanity during the Fall is brought to communion by the greatest sacrifice this world has ever known. May the flowers of your love—their beauty and fragrance—lead me to praise your name, to make your love known to all as an instrument of your love for all humanity. I ask all of this in the name of your Son, our Lord Jesus Christ. Amen.

ADVENT ACTION

Beginning today and continuing throughout the coming week, make it a point to say "thank you" to God for all the gifts he has given you. Thank God for any or all that apply from the following categories: family, friends, health, talents, peace, joy, happiness, rest, learning, and any others you can think of. Thank God especially for the gift of his Son made to you and all the world on Christmas Day.

The Lord adorns your life with great gifts and leads you down a path toward eternal life that is decorated with flowers of every kind and color. Make it a point to say "thank you" to all those people who have come into your life as a gift from God. Over the next week, make it a point to reach out to as many of these people as you can—by phone, email, handwritten note, or in person—and say "thank you" to each one of them. Let everyone know how much they have meant to you and how much they continue to mean to you as a gift from the Father.

PART III

~~~

$\mathcal{F}$ORMATS
for
$\mathcal{N}$IGHTLY $\mathcal{P}$RAYER
and
$\mathcal{R}$EADING

$\mathcal{T}$he purpose of presenting two optional formats for nightly reading and prayer is to offer ways to use the material in this book for group or individual prayer. Of course, there are other ways in which to use this book—for example, as a meditative daily reader or as a guide for a prayer journal—but the following familiar liturgical formats provide a structure that can be used in a variety of contexts.

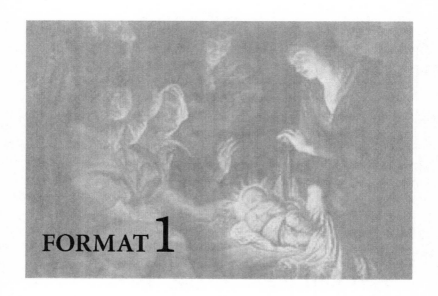

FORMAT 1

OPENING PRAYER

The observance begins with these words:

God, come to my assistance.

Lord, make haste to help me.

Followed by:

Glory be to the Father, the Son, and the Holy Spirit;

as it was in the beginning, is now, and ever shall be,

world without end. Amen.

EXAMINATION OF CONSCIENCE

If this observance is being prayed individually, an examination of conscience may be included. Here is a short examination of conscience; you may, of course, use your own method.

1. Place yourself in a quiet frame of mind.

2. Review your life since your last confession.

3. Reflect on the Ten Commandments and any sins against them.

4. Reflect on the words of the Gospel, especially Jesus' commandment to love your neighbor as yourself.

5. Ask yourself these questions:

- Have I been unkind in thoughts, words, and actions?

- Am I refusing to forgive anyone?

- Do I despise any group or person?

- Am I a prisoner of fear, anxiety, worry, guilt, inferiority, or self-hatred?

PENITENTIAL ACT (OPTIONAL)

If a group prays in unison, a penitential rite from *The Roman Missal* may be used:

Presider: You were sent to heal the contrite of heart: Lord, have mercy

All: Lord, have mercy.

Presider: You came to call sinners: Christ have mercy.

All: Christ, have mercy.

Presider: You are seated at the right hand of the Father to intercede for us: Lord, have mercy.

All: Lord, have mercy.

Presider: May almighty God have mercy on us, forgive us our sins, and bring us to everlasting life.

All: Amen.

HYMN: "O COME, O COME, EMMANUEL"

A hymn is now sung or recited. This Advent hymn is a paraphrase of the great "O" Antiphons, written in the twelfth century and translated by John Mason Neale in 1852.

O come, O come, Emmanuel,
And ransom captive Israel;
That mourns in lonely exile here,
Until the son of God appear.

Refrain: Rejoice! Rejoice! Emmanuel
        shall come to you, O Israel!

O come, O wisdom from on high,
Who orders all things mightily;
To us the path of knowledge show,
And teach us in her ways to go. (*Refrain*)

O come, O come, great Lord of might,
Who to your tribes on Sinai's height
In ancient times once gave the law,
In cloud, and majesty, and awe. (*Refrain*)

O come, O rod of Jesse's stem,
From ev'ry foe deliver them
That trust your mighty pow'r to save,
And give them vict'ry o'er the grave. (*Refrain*)

O come, O key of David, come,
And open wide our heav'nly home;
Make safe the way that leads on high,
And close the path to misery. (*Refrain*)

O come, O Dayspring from on high
And cheer us by your drawing nigh;
Disperse the gloomy clouds of night,
And death's dark shadow put to flight. (*Refrain*)

O come, Desire of nations, bind
In one the hearts of humankind;
O bid our sad divisions cease
And be for us our King of Peace. (*Refrain*)

PSALM 27:7–14 GOD STANDS BY US IN DANGERS

Hear my voice, LORD when I call;
have mercy on me and answer me.
"Come," says my heart, "seek his face";
your face, LORD, do I seek!
Do not hide your face from me;
do not repel your servant in anger.
You are my salvation; do not cast me off;
do not forsake me, God my savior!
Even if my father and mother forsake me,
the LORD will take me in.

LORD, show me your way;
lead me on a level path
because of my enemies.
Do not abandon me to the desire of my foes;
malicious and lying witnesses have risen against me.
I believe I shall see the LORD goodness
in the land of the living.
Wait for the LORD, take courage;
be stouthearted, wait for the LORD!

RESPONSE

I long to see your face, O Lord.
you are my light and my help
Do not turn away from me.

SCRIPTURE READING

Read silently or have preside proclaim the Scripture of the day that
is selected.

RESPONSE

Come and set us free, Lord God of power and might.
Let your face shine on us and we will be saved.

*Glory be to the Father, the Son, and the Holy Spirit;
as it was in the beginning, is now, and ever shall be,
world without end. Amen.*

SECOND READING

Read silently or have presider read the words of St. Thérèse for the day selected.

CANTICLE OF SIMEON (LUKE 2:29–32)

Now, Master, you may let your servant go in peace,
according to your word,
for my eyes have seen your salvation,
which you prepared in sight of all the peoples,
a light for revelation to the Gentiles,
and glory for your people Israel.

Glory be to the Father, the Son, and the Holy Spirit;
as it was in the beginning, is now, and ever shall be,
world without end. Amen.

PRAYER

Recite the prayer that follows the excerpt from St. Thérèse for the day selected.

BLESSING

May the all-powerful Lord grant us a restful night and a peaceful death. Amen.

MARIAN ANTIPHON

O loving Mother of our Redeemer,
    gate of heaven, star of the sea,
Hasten to aid thy fallen people
    who strive to rise once more.

Thou who brought forth thy holy Creator,
    all creation wond'ring,
Yet remainest ever Virgin,
    taking from Gabriel's lips that joyful "Hail!":
    be merciful to us sinners.

FORMAT 2

OPENING PRAYER

The observance begins with these words:

God come to my assistance.
Lord make haste to help me.

Followed by:

Glory be to the Father, the Son, and the Holy Spirit;
as it was in the beginning, is now, and ever shall be,
world without end. Amen.

EXAMINATION OF CONSCIENCE

If this observance is being prayed individually, an examination of conscience may be included. Here is a short examination of conscience; you may, of course, use your own method.

1. Place yourself in a quiet frame of mind.

2. Review your life since your last confession.

3. Reflect on the Ten Commandments and any sins against them.

4. Reflect on the words of the Gospel, especially Jesus' commandment to love your neighbor as yourself.

5. Ask yourself these questions:

- Have I been unkind in thoughts, words, and actions?

- Am I refusing to forgive anyone?

- Do I despise any group or person?

- Am I a prisoner of fear, anxiety, worry, guilt, inferiority, or self-hatred?

PENITENTIAL ACT (OPTIONAL)

If a group of people are praying in unison, a penitential rite from *the Roman Missal* may be used:

All: I confess to almighty God

and to you, my brothers and sisters,

that I have greatly sinned,

in my thoughts and in my words,

in what I have done and in what I have failed to do,

And, striking their breast they say:

through my fault, through my fault,

through my most grievous fault;

Then they continue:

therefore I ask blessed Mary ever-Virgin,

all the Angels and Saints,

and you, my brothers and sisters,
to pray for me to the Lord our God.

Presider: Have mercy on us, O Lord.

All: For we have sinned against you.

Presider: Show us, O Lord, your mercy.

All: And grant us your salvation.

HYMN: "BEHOLD A ROSE"

A hymn is now sung or recited. This traditional hymn was composed in German in the fifteenth century. It is sung to the melody of the familiar "Lo, How a Rose E're Blooming."

Behold, a rose of Judah
From tender branch has sprung,
From Jesse's lineage coming,
As men of old have sung.
It came a flower bright
Amid the cold of winter
When half spent was the night.

Isaiah has foretold it
In words of promise sure,
And Mary's arms enfold it,
A virgin meek and pure.
Through God's eternal will
She bore for men a savior
At midnight calm and still.

PSALM 40:2–8 THANKSGIVING FOR DELIVERANCE

Surely, I wait for the LORD;

who bends down to me and hears my cry,

Draws me up from the pit of destruction,

out of the muddy clay,

Sets my feet upon rock,

steadies my steps,

And puts a new song in my mouth,

a hymn to our God.

Many shall look on in fear,

and they shall trust in the LORD.

Blessed the man who sets his security in the LORD,

who turns not to the arrogant

or to those who stray after falsehood.

you, yes you, O LORD, my God,

have done many wondrous deeds!

And in your plans for us

there is none to equal you.

Should I wish to declare or tell them,

too many are they to recount.

Sacrifice and offering you do not want;

you opened my ears.

Holocaust and sin-offering you do not request;

so I said, "See; I come

with an inscribed scroll written upon me.

I delight to do your will, my God;

your law is in my inner being!"

RESPONSE

> May all who seek after you be glad in the Lord,
> may those who find your salvation say with continuous praise,
> "Great is the Lord!"

SCRIPTURE READING

Read silently or have a preside proclaim the Scripture of the day that is selected.

RESPONSE

> Lord, you who were made obedient unto death, teach us to always do the Father's will so that, sanctified by the holy obedience that joins us to your sacrifice, we can count on your immense love in times of sorrow.

> *Glory be to the Father, the Son, and the Holy Spirit;*
> *as it was in the beginning, is now, and ever shall be,*
> *world without end. Amen.*

SECOND READING

Read silently or have a preside read the words of St. Thérèse for the day selected.

CANTICLE OF SIMEON (LUKE 2:29–32)

Now, Master, you may let your servant go
in peace, according to your word,
for my eyes have seen your salvation,
which you prepared in sight of all the peoples,
a light for revelation to the Gentiles,
and glory for your people Israel.

Glory be to the Father, the Son, and the Holy Spirit;
as it was in the beginning, is now, and ever shall be,
world without end. Amen.

PRAYER

Recite the prayer that follows the excerpt from St. Thérèse for the
day selected.

BLESSING

Lord, give our bodies restful sleep and let the work we have
done today bear fruit in eternal life. Watch over us as we rest
in your peace. Amen.

MARIAN ANTIPHON

Hail, holy Queen, mother of mercy,
our life, our sweetness, and our hope.
To you do we cry,
poor banished children of Eve.
To you do we send up our sighs,
mourning and weeping in this vale of tears.

Turn then, most gracious advocate,
your eyes of mercy toward us,
and after this exile
show to us the blessed fruit of your womb, Jesus.
O clement, O loving,
O sweet Virgin Mary. Amen.

CPSIA information can be obtained at www.ICGtesting.com
Printed in the USA
LVOW06s1236170915

454567LV00003B/5/P